## DATE DUE

Demco, Inc. 38-293

JUN 0 6 2011

# Praise for
## *The Definitive Guide to HR Communication*

"Davis and Shannon make a compelling case for the value of simple, straightforward, and effective HR communication—and provide valuable insight on how to make it happen in even the most complex organizations."

> —**Kevin Kelly**, 30+ years internal communications veteran

"*The Definitive Guide to HR Communication* is a terrific resource for HR professionals. The examples and illustrations reflect actual issues and challenges we face and are a good reminder of how easily we can disconnect with our audience. The tips, tools, and guidelines are clear and effective in demonstrating alternative approaches to generating employee interest and understanding. I enjoyed reading it, found it very helpful, and have already begun using some of the suggested methods."

> —**Diane F. Green**, Director of Staffing and Development,
> Hollingsworth & Vose Company

"Don't be misled by the title of this book. It doesn't matter if you work in HR communications or not, you can learn from this well-written guide. In fact, even if you're not particularly interested in communications, you'll benefit from it . . . the book is *that* good.

"Here's why: The authors use a combination of stories, solid writing, checklists, and examples to lead even the greenest communicator through the steps of communicating to an audience. Even if you've been in the communications business as long as I have (more than 30 years!), you can still learn—or relearn—a thing or two. The book is organized so you can find what you need and use what you find.

"The authors freely borrow from the best, including communications guru Don Ranly. And, one of their great ideas is to 'Go Hollywood.' This is a technique to distill your message into a bite-sized chunk for today's busy workers. I tried it. It works. And, with a name like 'Go Hollywood,' the technique also is memorable.

"That's just one of the easy-to-implement techniques in this book. There are many. I was just a few pages in when I found something solid I could use at work . . . right now. I continued to read, marked up the pages, turned down the corners, and went back to the book again and again.

"Invest in this book. Your boss will wonder how you got so smart overnight!"

> —**Becky Healy**, Agency Communications Manager,
> State Farm Insurance, and 2010-2011 President,
> Council of Communication Management

"This book truly is a definitive guide to increasing employee engagement by helping people understand and appreciate their pay and benefits. Davis and Shannon's book should be invaluable to a range of business professionals: 1) From students who are learning the basics of employee engagement and talent management, to 2) HR and communication professionals who design and explain pay and benefits to employees, to 3) Managers and executives who sign off on people management strategies.

"The book is built on the premise that great benefits must be understood and appreciated if they are to be of real value. Davis and Shannon's book is all about helping organizations of every size get the most 'bang' for the expensive bucks they shell out on total rewards. The book starts with an analysis of how employees read and listen (or don't) and progresses through an analysis of what it takes to communicate effectively, including developing strategies, messaging, and media.

"Davis and Shannon follow their own advice. Their prose is straightforward and makes it easy for the reader to pay attention. Their examples are meaningful and come from real companies that have struggled with HR communication; the authors explain how some have failed and others have succeeded brilliantly. Their advice is thoughtful and reflects years of practical experience designing and producing award-winning HR communications. There are no two communicators who know more about this subject than Davis and Shannon—who better to write the definitive guide?"

—**Kate Nelson**, Faculty, Fox School of Business, Temple University


"Alison and Jane have put together a must-have resource for any Human Resources leader or professional who is involved with preparing company-wide communication events, or for those who coach those who put on these kinds of events. Written in a clear, easy-to-read format, you will find practical steps, real life examples, and realistic suggestions that, if followed, will dramatically improve the success of your communication events. Take the time to digest this book, follow the advice, and you will see measurable improvement in an area that has been difficult to get right for many organizations. Well done, Alison and Jane."

—**William G. Bliss**, President, Bliss & Associates Inc.,
and author, *Advisory Services to Cultivate*
*Exceptional Leadership*

# THE DEFINITIVE GUIDE TO HR COMMUNICATION

# THE DEFINITIVE GUIDE TO HR COMMUNICATION

## Engaging Employees in Benefits, Pay, and Performance

Alison Davis and Jane Shannon

Vice President, Publisher: Tim Moore
Associate Publisher and Director of Marketing: Amy Neidlinger
Executive Editor: Jeanne Glasser
Editorial Assistant: Pamela Boland
Development Editor: Russ Hall
Operations Manager: Gina Kanouse
Senior Marketing Manager: Julie Phifer
Publicity Manager: Laura Czaja
Assistant Marketing Manager: Megan Colvin
Cover Designer: Chuti Prasertsith
Managing Editor: Kristy Hart
Project Editor: Anne Goebel
Copy Editor: Gayle Johnson
Proofreader: Linda Seifert
Indexer: Erika Millen
Senior Compositor: Gloria Schurick
Manufacturing Buyer: Dan Uhrig

FT Press offers excellent discounts on this book when ordered in quantity for bulk purchases or special sales. For more information, please contact U.S. Corporate and Government Sales, 1-800-382-3419, corpsales@pearsontechgroup.com. For sales outside the U.S., please contact International Sales at international@pearson.com.

Second Printing March 2011

ISBN-10: 0-13-706143-9
ISBN-13: 978-0-13-706143-3

Pearson Education LTD.
Pearson Education Australia PTY, Limited.
Pearson Education Singapore, Pte. Ltd.
Pearson Education Asia, Ltd.
Pearson Education Canada, Ltd.
Pearson Educación de Mexico, S.A. de C.V.
Pearson Education—Japan
Pearson Education Malaysia, Pte. Ltd.

*Library of Congress Cataloging-in-Publication Data*

Davis, Alison, 1957-
  The definitive guide to HR communication : engaging employees in benefits, pay, and performance / Alison Davis, Jane Shannon.
    p. cm.
  ISBN 978-0-13-706143-3 (hbk. : alk. paper)
 1. Communication in personnel management. 2. Personnel management. I. Shannon, Jane, 1943- II. Title.
  HF5549.5.C6D36 2011
  658.30014—dc22

                        2010041782

*To my wonderful family, especially my husband and kids (and their significant others). You make me laugh and make all the hard work worthwhile.*
—*Alison Davis*

*To my son Lindsay, my daughter-in-law Joanne, and my grandsons Nolan and Dempsey Shannon. I love you guys!*
—*Jane Shannon*

# Table of Contents

# Acknowledgments

Inspiration about great communication is everywhere, and I've learned so much just by paying attention to the smart, talented people I work with, especially the terrific team at Davis & Company and our wonderful clients. As Yogi Berra once said, "You can see a lot just by looking," especially when you're surrounded by people doing great things.

Although I can't mention all these folks by name (that would fill the whole book), I would like to acknowledge my coauthor, Jane Shannon. She's one of the best writers on the planet and is a constant source of inspiration and delight.

—Alison Davis

First, thank you to my parents, Evelyn Lyon Risdon and James W. Risdon, who, among many achievements, both graduated from the University of Missouri School of Journalism and thus paved a trail that I followed.

Dr. Paul Fisher taught us the rules of typography and magazine design and then ended the semester by showing us how to break those rules effectively. Specifically, he demonstrated how collaboration between writer and graphic designer could lead to something greater than either could achieve alone.

Dr. Don Ranly, professor emeritus at the University of Missouri School of Journalism, will always be my favorite professor whose class I didn't attend (because I graduated before he began teaching). At least I was able to introduce him to my students when I taught at Mizzou as a visiting professor.

Thank you to all the wonderful colleagues, friends, and clients I've had the privilege to work with. Special thanks to Bettina Rounds, Alan Beechey, Kate Nelson, Ellen Blitz, Bob Warkulwiz, Peter Moore, David Eccles, Lief Skoogfors, Jim Jarrett, Peter Ross, and Craig Bernhardt.

Special thanks also go to Alison Davis as a friend, consultant, boss, colleague, and collaborator, and someone who always makes my work better. She's also the instigator of the great idea of creating this book.

Finally, thank you to two professional associations that helped me build my career, recognized the quality of my work, and also gave me the opportunity to give back to my profession: the International Association of Business Communicators and the Council of Communication Management.

—Jane Shannon

# About the Authors

## Alison Davis

For the past 25 years, Alison Davis has been CEO of Davis & Company (www.davisandco.com). This firm has helped such companies as BNY Mellon, Georgia-Pacific, IKEA, Johnson & Johnson, MasterCard, and Merck reach, engage, and motivate their employees.

Davis is coauthor of *Your Attention, Please* (Adams Business, 2006) and a weekly web log, "Insights," at www.davisandco.com/blog. She frequently writes articles for leading business, communication, and HR publications and is a former online columnist for *The New York Times*.

Davis is a sought-after speaker on a variety of communication topics and issues. She speaks at 10 to 15 conferences a year for such organizations as the Society of Human Resources Management, the International Association of Business Communicators, The Conference Board, and The Arthur Page Society.

A former president of the Council of Communication Management, she is a member of that organization as well as the International Association of Business Communicators and the Public Relations Society of America.

Davis has a bachelor's degree in English from Rutgers University.

## Jane Shannon

For much of her career, Jane Shannon served as vice president of human resources communication at Citibank, New York, NY. She then worked as a senior communication consultant at Davis & Company and as a principal in the communication practice of William M. Mercer, Inc. She is currently an independent consultant (www.janeshannon.com). Her clients have included companies as diverse as Texaco, Barnes & Noble, Bank of America, Toys "R" Us, and United Distillers & Vintners.

Shannon is author of *73 Ways to Improve Your Employee Communication Program* (Davis & Company, 2002), which consistently ranks at the top of Amazon's search term "employee communication." She has spoken at many communication conferences hosted by the Council of Communication Management and the International Association of Business Communicators.

Shannon is a member and former board member of CCM and is a former member of the IABC, where she earned local, regional, and international awards. Her work has been recognized with awards from the American Institute for Graphic Arts, the New York Art Directors, and the Philadelphia Art Directors. Her work also has been featured in *Graphis* and *Communication Arts*.

Shannon earned a bachelor of journalism, majoring in advertising, at the University of Missouri-Columbia, where she recently returned to teach as part of the School of Journalism Visiting Professor Program.

# Introduction

## Effective HR Communication: How to Get Employees to Pay Attention, Understand What's Changing, and Take Action

Your company makes a big investment in designing benefits, pay, and policies to attract and retain the best employees. That's why it's so frustrating when employees don't understand their benefits—or worse, don't appreciate what's available to them.

Employee confusion about key HR issues is all too common. In fact, most employees report that they are dissatisfied with communication about benefits and programs. For example, a 2007 Prudential study[1] found that only 35% of employees rate benefits communication as "highly effective."

And there's a direct correlation between how well employees understand their benefits, pay, and policies and how much they value and use their benefits. So poor communication leads to low usage, and low usage leads to poor perception. For example, only 44% of employees in a 2009 MetLife study[2] reported being satisfied with their benefits.

This is obviously a problem. First, workers who aren't knowledgeable can't make smart decisions or take appropriate action. Second, the less they know about pay and benefits, the less satisfied they are.

The MetLife study discovered that 70% of employees who have a strong understanding are happy with those benefits, but when understanding is low, only 7% are satisfied.

What causes employee confusion? A big factor is **poor communication**. Most HR departments generate a steady flow of communication, but employees don't find it effective. In fact, only 33% of employees in the MetLife study strongly believed that current communications educated them effectively. What's even more surprising is that only 36% of *employers* think communication effectively educates workers.

## "Help!" Cry HR Managers

HR managers know that communication is a big challenge. We've spent the past couple of years traveling around the country, talking with HR managers about communication issues. Here's what they tell us:

- "We have so much information to get out to employees regarding benefits and other HR-related services. We use e-mail, desk drop, posters, an intranet site, and mailings to homes. People don't have time to read it! Then they call with big issues."
- "My biggest challenge is reaching employees who work out of town; they don't receive their mail for long periods of time and don't use computers."
- "I struggle to boil things down to a level everyone can understand."
- "It's so difficult to get the message across to people who won't read it. It's about benefits and they complain that it's too complicated. 'Just tell me what to do,' they say."
- "I want to engage more employees in learning more about their benefits and attending annual open enrollment sessions. How do I increase participation in info sessions?"
- "How can I provide benefit information or instructions to a group of employees who vary widely in their level of understanding?"

- "It's hard getting people to understand, not just listen—to get and keep their interest."
- "I find that employees don't read the materials. The information is too technical."
- "I find myself answering the same benefit questions over and over. Aargh!"

# Why Don't Employees Pay Attention?

In a way, confusion about HR programs is surprising: Since employees care deeply about these issues, you'd think they'd work hard to understand them. For example, in the MetLife study, employees say the most important factors affecting their loyalty to the company are

- Salary/wages (83% of employees agreed)
- Health benefits (75%)
- Retirement benefits (72%)

In fact, these priorities rank higher than advancement opportunities (57%) and company culture (50%).

In the past, employees would pay attention to any HR communication that came their way. Even if the communication was long, dense, and difficult to understand—for instance, a Summary Plan Description—employees would do the heavy lifting to make sense of it.

But times have changed. Benefits, pay, and retirement programs are more complex than ever before. And employees today simply don't have the time to hack their way through a thicket of information—even when the topic matters to them. They're quick to press the Delete key or file a message for future consideration or simply let it fall to the bottom of the pile. They wait until a deadline is looming—or until an issue is so urgent that it can't be ignored—before they read the message.

A number of factors can cause a breakdown in communication:

- **Information overload.** Workers are overwhelmed. For instance, the research firm Basex[3] estimates that 28%—more than one-fourth—of an average knowledge worker's day is taken up by managing unnecessary e-mail and instant messages. Another firm, RescueTime, calculates that a worker who sits at a computer all day turns to his e-mail program more than 50 times and uses instant messaging 77 times.

- **Complexity.** HR information used to be simple. There was one healthcare plan, one company-paid retirement program, and a few job-related policies. But today choices abound. Complexity is the order of the day. It's no wonder that 55% of U.S. healthcare plan members don't fully understand critical details about their insurance coverage, according to a 2008 study by J.D. Power and Associates.[4]

- **Employee attitudes.** In a business environment where layoffs occur often, it's no surprise that employees don't have the same sense of loyalty and connection to their companies as they used to. So they view any "corporate communication" not with enthusiasm, but with caution at best or skepticism and distrust at worst.

- **HR's reputation.** In many companies, employees have had negative experiences with HR—and with HR communication. For example, in focus groups we've conducted, we've heard employees give feedback like this:
  - "HR doesn't respect my time."
  - "HR communication includes way too much jargon."
  - "HR isn't interested in me; it's all about pleasing senior management and cutting costs."
  - "Here comes another takeaway."

# What's Wrong with This Picture?

Created (or at least approved) by subject-matter experts, HR communication often offers technical information in a dense and thorny presentation—a veritable maze of information. And when it's vetted by lawyers, you'll find caveats and disclaimers that create another barrier to understanding.

Perhaps even worse, most communication seems designed to appeal to management by using language and tone more suited to the corner office than to the cubicles where most employees work. As a result, employees tell us that too often they find communication confusing, inconvenient, irrelevant, and just plain annoying. They also say they're unclear about what action to take and how to get their questions answered.

## A Fresh Approach

It doesn't have to be this way. We've discovered that communication can meet all its obligations (to lawyers, the government, and company management) while appealing to employees. From decades of experience, we've developed a communication approach that interests employees, persuades them of the value of a program or policy, and helps them decide on the course of action that is best for them (and their company).

Our approach is simple: **treat employees as customers** of HR benefits and services. We use the same strategies, tools, and care your company uses to sell your products or services to your customers. We learn all we can about employees (age, years of service, education, job family, location, salary, and more), and we learn from employees themselves how, when, where, and from whom they like to receive information. We determine the specific information that employees need and when they need it. Then we package the information for them in ways that make it easy for them to understand and make good decisions in a timely way.

Here's an example of what we mean:

| BEFORE Here's what the client wrote: | AFTER Here's our edit: |
|---|---|
| In line with our company's increasing decentralization, enhanced processes and tools to support mobility are expected to increase staffing flexibility and improve opportunities for career growth. These enhancements include identifying staff members who are ready for mobility, providing greater transparency on opportunities and options for mobility and offering improved benefits for temporary assignments. | **Helping you build your career**<br>We're helping you build your career—while we're helping the company meet customer needs—with new ways to work, including temporary assignments, that will<br>• Identify when you're ready to move into a new job<br>• Communicate clearly and quickly your opportunities and options when you relocate<br>• Provide improved benefits when you take a temporary assignment |

When what you write (see BEFORE) sits there like a block of gray granite, it's hard to read, whether it's on the screen or in print. When the language isn't conversational—doesn't talk directly to the reader—it's harder to figure out "what it means to me" as the reader. Effective HR communication, on the other hand, makes information accessible, easy to understand, and useful.

As a result, employees know what they can expect from the company, and they know what the company expects of them.

When you create effective HR communication, you

- Help employees take advantage of all the benefits and programs the company offers
- Make it easy for employees to understand and use benefits and programs effectively
- Answer most of the questions employees have about company benefits, programs, and policies

# How This Book Can Help

This book shows you how to communicate differently and more effectively. Even if you're already doing a great job, we can help you improve.

First, we provide practical tips on how to take communication from boring to compelling. Then we give you advice on how to communicate in these common situations:

- Recruiting
- Orientation
- Policies
- Benefits
- Compensation
- Performance Management
- Saving for Retirement
- Leaving the Company

Along the way, we do the following:

- Supply evidence that will impress senior managers and convince them that you need to change your approach to engage employees successfully.
- Provide an approach that you can use every time you craft a brochure, web page, electronic newsletter, or even a brief e-mail.
- Give specific techniques for how to communicate in a more accessible way, including breaking your points into digestible chunks; signaling what is ahead in your text (with packaging devices such as subheads); and giving your audience all kinds of other tools—such as charts, checklists, and captions—that allow skimming and scanning.
- Show examples of good communication (and explain why it works) and bad (and offer advice on how to make it much better).
- Practice what we preach by demonstrating our strategies and techniques throughout the book.

We also bring in examples from real companies to make the business case that demonstrates how to communicate more effectively. As a result, you'll learn how to

- Communicate faster, more efficiently, and more effectively.
- Help employees take advantage of all the benefits the company offers.
- Make it easy for employees to understand and use benefits effectively.
- Answer most of the questions employees have.

# Doing It Right Means a Better Bottom Line

What's in it for your company if you read this book and follow the advice presented here?

The bottom line is simply this: **Good HR communication helps contribute to employee productivity, which in turn boosts your company's profitability.** There's a good reason to turn the page.

# Part I

## Taking a New Approach

# 1

# Know Your Employees

*In this chapter, you learn*

- *Why it's important to know your "employee audience"*
- *What demographics can reveal about employees*
- *How to learn more through focus groups and other qualitative research*

If you were to enroll in a college course on marketing, the very first rule you'd learn is this: "Know your audience." That's because the most effective way to reach people—and to motivate them to take action—is to understand who they are and what they need.

This may sound basic, but assessing employees is a step that's often skipped in HR communication. We plunge into creating communication without thinking about the people we're creating it for. Even worse, we assume that employees are just like us, taking for granted that the ways *we* like communicating will work equally well for employees in a variety of jobs, geographies, and functions.

Like many assumptions, this one is dangerous. It leads to these kinds of communication mistakes:

- Using terms such as "competencies" and "salary structure" that make perfect sense to HR experts but that mean nothing to employees.
- Telling the entire history of how a program was developed, when employees just want to know what's changed and what they need to do about it.

- Failing to make connections or put topics in context. You know that "compensation" consists of different elements such as base pay, bonuses, and stock options, but employees may not understand that the individual pieces add up to something called "compensation."

---

*"People only understand things in terms of their experience, which means that you must get within their experience."*

—Saul D. Alinsky, *Rules for Radicals: A Pragmatic Primer for Realistic Radicals*[1]

---

How can you make sure you truly know your employee audience? We recommend that you start by analyzing your **employee demographics** and then conducting **qualitative research**—such as focus groups—to explore communication needs and preferences. This chapter shows you how.

# What Demographics Can Reveal About Employees

Back when we started our careers (a long, long time ago), the subject of demographics rarely came up, mostly because there was very little to talk about. After all, the employees at most U.S. companies were mostly homogenous: mostly male, mostly white, mostly all from the same region, with similar backgrounds, accents, values, and aspirations.

Obviously, the workforce has changed. For example, in the United States, the newest generation entering the employment market, the Millennials (born between 1980 and 2000), represents a much more diverse group than the previous two generations. Some 40% of Millennials are black, Latino, or Asian, compared with a total of 25% in both of the previous two generations (Generation X and the baby boomers).

This is just one reason why it's become so crucial to conduct an analysis of your workforce demographics periodically.

**dem-o-graph-ics**

The characteristics of human populations and population segments, especially when used to identify consumer markets: *The demographics of the Southwest indicate a growing population of older consumers.*

—Houghton Mifflin dictionary

# What You Can Learn from Demographics

Demographics offer a way to distinguish and describe characteristics of a population to determine what sets that segment apart. Although not a foolproof predictor, demographics are so valuable that it's surprising that HR professionals don't always have employee information at their fingertips. Everyone typically knows how many employees work at their company, but you also need to know other important facts about your employees:

**Key employee demographics:**

- **Where** are your employees located?
- What is the average length of **employee service**?
- How are your employees divided in terms of **age**? **Male/female ratio**? **Ethnic mix**? **Educational level**?
- What is the median **salary** for all employees? What are the salary ranges for different job families, businesses, and locations?
- How many employees fall into each **pay/job grade** or **job/functional category**?
- Which primary **languages** do your employees speak? For what percentage of your employee audience is English a second language?

- How many employees support **dependents**? On average, how many dependents do they have?
- How many employees have **computers** at work, easy access to the company intranet, and e-mail accounts?
- Can employees take time at work to **attend meetings about HR programs**, services, and products? Do meetings need to be held before or after work or at lunchtime? Do employees need to be paid overtime to attend these meetings?
- What percentage of your employee population belongs to a **union**? How many unions are represented at your workplace?
- How many employees are also **customers** of your company? How many are also shareholders in your company?

Your employee demographics will give you valuable insights into almost every aspect of communication, especially the following:

- **What** to communicate (content) and what examples will resonate with your audience.
- **How** to communicate (for example, print, electronic, or face-to-face).
- **When** and **where** to communicate.

For example, your company's medical plan enrollments will show you what percentage of your population has children. This is important to know when you're communicating about many topics, such as medical benefits, life insurance, savings, time off, and flexible work arrangements. Understanding how many employees have families also helps you know when to communicate. For example, meetings before or after work may be difficult for some employees to attend.

---

*"Demographics explain about two-thirds of everything."*

—David K. Foot, professor of economics at the University of Toronto and author of *Boom, Bust & Echo: Profiting from the Demographic Shift in the 21st Century*[2]

---

## Learning from Key Facts

Here's an example of how a demographic analysis can create insights about how to make communication more effective. (This is based on an actual company, but some of the facts have been changed to protect confidential information.)

At a global healthcare company, the Benefits and Compensation group asked the Payroll department to provide a demographic report (which in this company was called a "headcount report") on employees.

Here is what Payroll provided:

| | |
|---|---|
| Global employees | 25,164 |
| U.S. employees | 13,043 |
| | |
| Exempt U.S. | 9,133 |
| Exempt non-U.S. | 7,782 |
| | |
| Nonexempt U.S. | 3,910 |
| Nonexempt non-U.S. | 4,339 |
| | |
| Employees in corporate | 322 |
| Division 1 | 1,550 |
| Division 2 | 1,716 |
| Division 3 | 21,576 |
| | |
| U.S. employees earning less than $70,000 | 7,229 |

This data is hardly exhaustive, but the Benefits and Compensation manager still learned a few things from these demographics:

- Nearly half the employees work outside the United States. That means it's likely that a portion of these employees speak English as a second language (or don't speak English at all); therefore, communication needs to be simple, and some messages may need to be translated.

*continued*

- A small percentage of employees (1.2%) work in corporate headquarters. There's often an inclination to design communication to appeal to internal clients at corporate (including senior management), but doing so may mean it doesn't meet the needs of the majority of employees.

- Since Division 3 is disproportionately large, it may get the lion's share of attention. But the communication needs of employees in the other two divisions must be considered as well.

- There's a bit of interesting information about income (55% of U.S. employees earn less than $70,000), which may be useful in thinking about communicating compensation and certain benefits. It may be even more helpful to obtain a more comprehensive breakdown of income levels, if Payroll has the data available.

# Four Key Demographics to Explore

Are you ready to take a closer look at your company's employee demographics? Since most of us have limited time and budgets, we can't consider every detail. But you should think about four critical categories: geography, years of service, age, and salary.

## Geography

Even in this age where electronic communication breaks down boundaries, geography still matters. Where a person lives and works rates as an important part of his or her identity.

**Gather the following demographic data on geography:**

- Your organization's geographic scope: Pinpoint all the locations on a map of the country or the globe, and see how your organization is distributed.

- The number of employees who work at headquarters and other major locations.

- Remote locations: how many employees work at small facilities.

- Field employees (such as sales representatives), work-from-home employees, and client-located employees.

## *Years of Service*

How long employees stay with an organization has both practical and cultural implications. A stable employee population has a long memory, which can be a positive (strong company heritage) or a negative (still seething over something that happened years ago). By contrast, if turnover is high, employees need to ramp up quickly on procedures and culture, and this information needs to be refreshed frequently.

**Gather the following demographic data on tenure:**

| Length of Service | Percentage of Employees |
|---|---|
| Less than 1 year | |
| 1 to 3 years | |
| 3+ to 10 years | |
| 10+ to 20 years | |
| 20+ years | |

## The 401(k) Challenge

A potential client once asked us for recommendations on how the company (a warehouse-type retail operation) could get higher participation in its 401(k) savings plan.

After asking a few questions about employee demographics, we learned that most of the company's employees were young, received minimum wage, and didn't stay with the company for the required one year of service needed to be able to participate in the 401(k) plan.

With demographics like that, it would take a lot more than a memorable communications campaign to boost participation numbers. Automatic enrollment at date of hire (plus some kind of company

match) could raise the percentage of participating employees—
but to what avail if most were leaving before a single year of
employment?

This is also a great example of a "communication challenge" that
actually is a problem that communications probably can't fix.
Before launching into any new programs to increase 401(k) participation, this company needs to find out why employees are
leaving before completing a year of service, and what, if anything, the company can do to reverse this trend.

## Age

Here's a demographic term for you: "generational cohort." This is
"the aggregation of individuals who experience the same event within
the same time interval." Sociologists and marketers use terms such as
"baby boomers" and "Gen Xers" to describe groups of people bound
together by broad shared experience.

This is important for two reasons:

1. Our attitudes are informed by how old we are and by the generation in which we grew up, including the movies we saw, the
   music we listened to, and the world events we witnessed.

2. How people experience communication continues to be influenced by age.

For example, many baby boomers who remember where they
were when President Kennedy was shot vividly recall all those work-
days before computers and e-mail (the days of the printed memo).
Many still aren't completely comfortable with the latest in technology.
Workers younger than 40 grew up using technology, and most master
new channels with ease.

## Gather the following demographic data on age:

| Birth Years | Generational Cohort |
| --- | --- |
| Before 1945 | Seniors (also known as the Greatest Generation and the Silent Generation) |
| 1946 to 1964 | Baby boomers |
| 1965 to 1980 | Generation X |
| 1980 to 2000 | Millennials |

## *Salary*

Along with geography, age, and years of service, salary also ranks as an important demographic, especially when you're communicating about any financially based plans, such as savings plans, retirement plans, or stock purchase plans.

You'll want to show examples of how these plans would work for people earning at various salary levels. It's a good rule of thumb to show examples beginning with a number less than the low end of your company's salary ranges and then include numbers that can easily be multiplied for your top earners. There's no need to reinforce pay differences between lower-level workers and executives. You should show how everyone, no matter what his or her salary is, can participate in savings and other financial plans.

### Gather the following demographic data on salary:

- Percentage of workers paid by the hour. Depending on your company, you may have different levels of hourly workers. For example, retail employees are often paid near minimum wage, so their pay is much lower than experienced hourly workers at a unionized manufacturing plant.
- Percentage of exempt salaried workers.
- Employees in various nonexempt bands, from new hires to executives.

## A Detailed Profile

At a telecommunications company, we worked with HR and employee communication teams to develop a comprehensive analysis of employee demographics by division. Here's an overview of the data:

| Division | Consumer | Business | Network |
|---|---|---|---|
| **Number of Employees** | 3,100 | 1,500 | 8,600 |
| **Geography** | 18 locations | 23 locations | 19 locations |
| | 65% of employees are in OH, MI, MN | 70% of employees are in KS, NE, MN | 47% of employees are in OH and MN |
| **Jobs/Levels** | 15% exempt | 53% exempt | 20% exempt |
| | 75% nonexempt | 47% nonexempt | 17% nonexempt |
| | 10% union | 72% in customer-facing jobs | 63% union |
| | 67% in customer-facing jobs | | 61% in customer-facing jobs |
| **Average Age** | 37 | 44 | 49 |
| **Average Length of Service** | 7 years | 12 years | 22 years |
| **Gender** | 58% male, 42% female | 36% male, 64% female | 79% male, 21% female |

Since this data is more complete, it offers a number of insights:

- Employees in the Network division are older, have the longest length of service in the company, belong to a union, and are predominantly male. These guys are likely to prefer print communication over electronic channels.

- The Business division is a different story: It is mostly exempt employees, and mostly female. These employees use a computer every day for work but may have limited time while on the job to pay attention to HR communication, since they're interacting with customers.

- In all three divisions, in fact, the majority of employees are customer-facing. This limits the amount of time they can spend on communication.

- Geography is a factor: Employees are spread out across many different locations throughout the Midwest. That makes face-to-face communication challenging, but it can be worth the investment if the issues are important enough.

# Use Focus Groups to Explore Needs and Preferences

As you can tell, we're big fans of demographics, agreeing with David Foot that they explain "two-thirds of everything." But to really get inside the minds of employees, you need to go further and talk to them. The best way to do so is to conduct focus groups.

Why focus groups? This proven research method—widely practiced by marketers, scientists, and other professionals since the 1920s—can help you do the following:

- Explore an issue.
- Test a concept.
- Follow up on the launch of a program to see how well it was understood or received.
- Find out why employees answered a survey in a certain way.

Focus groups are a form of qualitative research that explores an issue in depth, allowing people to express their opinions and engage in dialog. Unlike quantitative research (such as surveys), qualitative research does not provide statistical data. Yet qualitative research is considered a scientifically valid tool that yields valuable insights into what people perceive and believe.

In addition to focus groups, types of qualitative research include one-on-one interviews (often used when the topic is personal or sensitive, or when it's logistically difficult to bring people together) and user testing (observing a person while he or she completes a task, such as visiting a website or completing a form).

Focus groups are ideal when you need to explore a topic in an open-ended way, since you can dive deeper and ask follow-up questions. If you need to ask, "Why is this true?" or "What does this mean?", focus groups are the right research method.

Although focus groups can seem deceptively simple to manage—"All you need to do is gather employees in a conference room and start talking, right?"—experts know that this research method is more complicated than meets the eye. That's why HR professionals often turn to research firms or external moderators to assist with focus group studies.

## *Guidelines for Conducting Focus Groups*

If you decide to manage your own focus groups, several good books provide how-to information:

*The Focus Group Kit* by David L. Morgan and Richard A. Krueger (Sage Publications, 1997)

*How to Conduct Employee Focus Groups* by Joe DeLuccia, Kimberly Gavagan, and David Pitre (Davis & Company, 2009)

*Moderating Focus Groups: A Practical Guide for Group Facilitation* by Dr. Thomas L. Greenbaum (Sage Publications, 1999)

We can't give you a complete recipe for conducting focus groups. But we believe three factors will help you plan a focus group study: set objectives, develop a discussion guide, and choose participants.

### *Set Objectives*

Your first step is to set objectives, which articulate—in a disciplined, focused way—what you're trying to learn as a result of your focus group research. Objectives provide a framework to answer the question: What am I willing and able to change as a result of this research?

Setting objectives begins with creating a thesis, a statement that summarizes what you're trying to accomplish.

The thesis can be expressed as statement ("Employees seem to be just going through the motions in the performance management system, instead of participating fully.") or as a question ("How will employees react to the new retirement program?"). In either case, the thesis articulates the core reason you're engaging in focus groups.

After you've nailed down the thesis, use it to create no more than three objectives.

### Executive Compensation

An HR team created the following research thesis: "We suspect that leaders don't understand how compensation works. Is that true, and, if so, how does that lack of understanding affect leaders' perception of the pay system?"

The team then developed these objectives for a focus group study:

- Determine how well leaders understand the compensation program overall.
- Assess the perceived value of specific components.
- Test and validate new plan concepts.

### *Develop a Discussion Guide*

As soon as your objectives are set, you're ready to develop a discussion guide, which is the term used by researchers to describe the document—part script, part outline—that the focus group moderator uses to facilitate the session.

To create a discussion guide, think about the two or three main things you want to learn. For example, if your thesis involves finding out what employees think about a change to disability plans, you could explore these categories:

- Employees' understanding of the current plans
- Their reaction to planned changes
- How they would like to learn about changes

Once you have your main categories, think about the key questions for each category that will help your moderator discuss the issue with participants. Avoid the temptation to create a long list of questions. The idea is to give the moderator a sense of structure, not to script every word he or she will say.

## Sample Discussion Guide

The following is an example of a simple discussion guide used in a one-hour focus group designed to explore how employees were perceiving the current HR program.

### Study Objectives:

Inquire about HR communication needs and preferences, find out how employees are using the HR website, and get employee reaction to recent communication regarding the new benefits plan.

### Discussion Outline:

### A. Introduction/manage expectations

- Explain why the focus group is being held, along with ground rules for participation and what to expect.

### B. HR information needs and preferences

- How do you currently get information about benefits and other HR programs and policies?
- Do you feel well-informed about your benefits?
- What would you like more information about?

### C. Use of HR website

- Do you currently use the company's HR website?
- What do you use it for?
- Do you find the information useful?
- What, if anything, would you change about the site?

### D. Reaction to recent HR communication

- Did you receive the recent message from HR about the new medical plan?
- What was your reaction to the message?
- How did it make you feel?
- What, if anything, would you change about similar messages in the future?

### E. Close

- Thank you/next steps.

*Choose Participants*

Most focus studies involve a limited number of participants. For example, even a large study might engage fewer than 100 people from an overall workforce of 10,000 employees. Because the sample is so small, it's critical to be smart about how participants are selected and to work hard to encourage selected employees to participate.

The best way to select participants is to use a method called "purposively selected" sampling. This consists of deciding on your criteria and then finding people who meet these criteria. This is different from the random sampling used for surveys, and it's a far cry from the casual way in which focus groups are often put together—inviting only people you know.

For example, if your thesis is "How do employees regard the current benefits program?", your sample would be benefits-eligible employees. You then can decide if you'd like to segment subgroups. When Alison's firm conducted focus groups to gather feedback on an executive pay program, the sample was all executives, but participants were grouped by level: junior and intermediate executives into one set of focus groups, and senior executives into another.

### Guidance on Selecting Participants

Using your demographic data as a foundation, answer these questions to jump-start your thinking about who should participate:

- How is your employee population structured? What are the main demographic groups? Do you need to segregate various sets of employees (manager/nonmanager, bands/levels, or new employees versus long-timers)?

- Where are your major locations? Should your sample reflect important differences between locations? For instance, do you have large facilities and small ones, locations in the United States and in other countries, warehouses versus retail establishments?

- What groups will your company management expect to see represented in order for them to feel comfortable about what you learn in the focus groups? Asking this question can potentially direct you to include a small but important employee group in your research.

First decide on criteria, and then find people who meet those criteria.

# Checklist for Knowing Your Employees

✓ Consider who's in your employee audience before beginning any communication program.

✓ Gather data on where your employees work to understand their geographic demographics.

✓ Use data about length of service to influence the depth of information you provide.

✓ Understand how "generational cohorts" shape how employees think, behave, and prefer to receive communication.

✓ Compile salary data to inform communication, especially about pay, savings, retirement, stock, and other financially based programs.

✓ Use focus groups or other qualitative research methods to explore employee attitudes, experiences, and preferences.

✓ Before conducting focus groups, be clear on the objectives of your research to ensure that your study is structured to achieve those objectives.

# 2

# Treat Your Employees Like Customers

*In this chapter, you learn*

- *What it means to treat your employees like customers, and why it's important to do so*
- *Four ways to use demographic information and research about your employees to communicate in a "customer-centric" way*

If you do just one thing differently as a result of reading this book, let it be this: **Treat your employees just like your customers.** Take this small step, and big, positive results will follow.

Here's why. Your company has many important constituents— from government regulators to unions, shareholders, customers, neighbors, and the press. Your employees occupy a unique place in this group.

When your employees do a great job, create new products, build your brand, and sell your wares, they also forge a positive link with one or more of the other groups important to your company's success.

Think about it, and you'll realize how appropriate it is to treat your employees like customers. They *are*, after all, customers of the HR benefits, services, and programs your company offers.

# How to Sell Employees on the Value of Working for Your Company

When Jane was hired to head up the HR communications unit at Citibank, her boss said, "We want you to use your background in advertising and marketing to sell employees on the value of working here." This was innovative in the late 1970s, and it would still be considered an innovative approach in many businesses today.

Yet it works. Whether you communicate electronically, in writing, or in person, treating employees like you treat your valued customers changes everything. It changes how you communicate, what you say, how you say it, and the results you get. In this chapter, we show you how to treat employees like customers of HR products and services, because that's precisely who they are.

Take a look at the marketing materials your company sends to customers or the financial communications you send to shareholders, and compare them to the HR communication materials your employees receive. Are they compatible in terms of quality? Tone? Clarity? If they aren't, how do you suppose employees interpret the difference?

# How Marketers Begin: By Knowing Their Customers

In Chapter 1, "Know Your Employees," we emphasized the importance of analyzing the demographics of your employees and using focus groups to determine their experiences, preferences, and needs. Now we show you how to use this new knowledge to design communication that meets employees' needs while accomplishing your objectives.

## Four Ways to Treat Your Employees Like Customers

If you want to treat your employees like customers, here are four steps you can take that will help you create effective HR communications:

1. Create a profile of your target "customers."

2. Assess the current state of employee understanding.

3. Build communication around employee preferences.

4. Make it easy for employees to do the right thing.

### Create a Profile of Your Target "Customers"

We're kind of geeky, so we love statistics. But it's not surprising that most HR professionals are less interested in math and more focused on people. That's why we often start communication planning by creating employee profiles.

### What's a Profile?

In marketing, "customer profile" can be briefly defined as "A precise description of the characteristics of buyers for a specific product or service." For a longer explanation, we like how Answers.com describes a customer profile:

> Description of a customer group or type of customer based on various demographic, psychographic and/or geographic characteristics; also called shopper profile. For example, magazine advertising salespeople provide advertisers with customer profiles describing the type of person who will be exposed to advertisements in that magazine. The description may include income, occupation, level of education, age, gender, hobbies, or area of residence. Customer profiles provide the knowledge needed to select the best prospect lists and to enable advertisers to select the best media.[1]

Why are profiles valuable? Product developers and marketers find them useful because they go beyond dry data to bring customers to life. When you can imagine the people you're trying to reach—with all their desires and preferences and quirks—you can do a better job of giving them what they need.

We find the same is true for HR. Profiles help us move from thinking abstractly about employees to seeing them as living, breathing people.

Although profiles are insightful, creating them doesn't have to be a long, drawn-out process. Our simple method goes like this: We ask our clients to pull all the demographic data available on their employees and bring it to a planning meeting. The most relevant facts are projected on a PowerPoint slide or posted on a flipchart.

## Employees at a Financial Company

When we facilitated a communication planning session at a financial company, our clients brought the following demographic information to the meeting (which we've altered slightly to share with you):

| Band | 1 | 2 | 3 | 4 |
|---|---|---|---|---|
| **Titles** | Nonexempt | Exempt and new managers | Experienced middle managers, directors | VPs and above |
| **Gender** | More female | More male | More female | More male |
| **Location(s)** | Orlando Rochester Edinburgh | Raleigh Ottawa | Chicago Schaumburg | Chicago |
| **Tenure** | 5 or more years | 5 or more years | 5 or more years | 5 or more years |
| **Business Area/ Function** | Middle markets Manufacturing | Middle markets Manufacturing | Finance Corporate functions | Finance or functions |

By reviewing this data, we could see many similarities among the groups—such as length of service—but also some important differences. For example, employees tended to be located in different areas depending on their level, and functions were also clustered by level.

To complement our client's demographic information, we bring our own contribution: a stack of stock photographs, each portraying a head-and-shoulders view of an individual. There's a photo of a 45-year-old man wearing a suit, for example, another of a 30-something woman who looks like she's driving a truck, and still another of a guy in his late 20s who works in IT support.

Based on the data, the entire group works together to decide on three or four key demographic segments we need to target with our upcoming communication.

We then break participants into small groups and ask each break-out team to take one demographic group and create a portrait of a typical employee in that segment, using one of the photos provided and a blank flipchart page.

## Profile

At the financial company mentioned in the preceding sidebar, our planning team used the demographic information they had brought—as well as feedback from focus groups—to develop four profile posters. Here is one of them:

***Poster 1:*** *Diane (Band 1)*

Top-of-Mind Concerns

- Diane is more focused on managing work/life than advancing her career.
- She takes pride in her work and worries about job security.

*continued*

Work at Our Company

- She is unsure whether she wants to be promoted, but she definitely wants to increase her salary.
- She would leave the firm if a competitor offered her higher pay for the same responsibilities.
- Her perceptions about the company are heavily influenced by her manager.

Knowledge of HR Policies and Programs

- Diane knows a lot about her benefits—because she uses health benefits for her family—but she knows less about compensation.
- She participates in performance management but closely follows the direction of her manager.

Channel/Vehicle Preferences

- Her preferred way to learn information is by meeting with her manager.
- She also relies on enrollment packages mailed to her home.
- She will look at the intranet if it has information she needs.

What do you do with profiles after you've developed them? Some people we know actually hang profile posters in their offices to keep the employee customer in view. Others include profiles in Power-Point presentations that describe employees—along with demographic data, engagement survey scores, and other information—that they use when presenting to peers or senior management about employees. Still others build profiles into communication plans—right after the section on objectives and before the part about strategies—to make sure their program is on target. Whatever you decide to do with the profiles you create, the idea is to make your employees as vivid as possible, and then make decisions about communication based on your new knowledge.

### Assess the Current State of Employee Understanding

A wise client once said to us, "Never underestimate employees' intelligence or overestimate their knowledge." We've kept that advice in mind ever since, especially when it comes to HR communication. You are probably a subject-matter expert on (or at least well-versed in) health benefits and/or performance objectives and/or variable compensation and/or short-term disability. But chances are that even your smartest employees have only superficial knowledge about any of these topics.

For example, we conducted focus groups for a consumer products company to find out what leaders understood (and thought about) a valuable but complicated executive pay program. The results? Leaders who participated admitted that they didn't really get it:

- "I've been here five years, and I'm still learning every day how this is structured and how it's weighted and the impact on me. I think it's too complicated."
- "I have difficulty understanding exactly how all of this adds up for me personally every year. This is very confusing."
- "I have the most complicated spreadsheet to manage my compensation. It has macros in it; it has all sorts of stuff just to manage how much money comes into my household. It's unbelievable."

This story illustrates that even when employees are highly intelligent (these executives are the best and the brightest in a very smart company) and the subject is something that matters to them (pay certainly ranks high in importance), there can still be significant gaps in what employees understand about an HR policy or program.

That's why we encourage you to use focus groups to assess your employees' knowledge thoroughly. Only by doing so can you design communication that effectively explains what employees need to know and do.

*Build Communication Around Employee Preferences*

Your company's marketing department spends a great deal of time and money to figure out which communication channels your customers read, watch, and listen to. And it also exhaustively tests potential messages to see which words, phrases, and images resonate with customers. Only when that analysis is complete does your marketing group create a communication program designed to reach and engage your customers.

Okay. You know where we're going here. Just do the same with your employees as you prepare HR communications.

You'll want to do the following:

- Conduct focus groups or other qualitative research before you begin your communications.
- Get feedback from employees on your HR communications after you have distributed them (see Chapter 9, "Measure Effectiveness").

By getting employee feedback before you create your communications plan and strategy, you'll learn the following:

- What employees like and don't like about a specific benefit.
- Questions employees typically have—or questions that vary based on demographics.
- Knowledge levels—what employees know, don't know, or the "facts versus fiction" of a particular benefit or program.
- Communication preferences—how employees prefer to hear about changes in their benefits or HR programs.
- Usage—who's using the benefit program, when, and why—and answers to the question, "Does usage vary by demographics?"

## What's the One Thing You Would Change?

If you can include one open-ended question in a survey or focus group, here is our recommendation for how to word it: "If you could change one thing about how we communicate HR policies, programs, and issues, what would it be?" We find that employees respond to this question by offering tangible suggestions for making communication better, many of which you can act on immediately to improve your program.

For example, we conducted an employee communication survey for a global industrial company, including our favorite query as the final question. Six hundred employees wrote down an answer, and when we analyzed the responses, we could see some key trends emerging:

| Number of Responses | Idea | Sample Quote |
|---|---|---|
| 55 | Be more transparent | "Eliminate the hidden agendas. Give it to me straight." |
| 42 | Make messages more relevant | "A lot of information is available, but it is difficult to tell what is meaningful to me personally." |
| 39 | Improve timeliness | "Provide more lead time when a change affects me personally." |
| 37 | Streamline communication | "Provide a summary of key communication, with links to enable further in-depth reading if employees need more detail." |

The first change we made as a result of these findings was that we helped our clients make messages clearer and more personally relevant and useful. We discuss how to do so in Chapters 4, "Frame Your Message," and 5, "Write Simply and Clearly."

*Make It Easy for Employees to Do the Right Thing*

Most companies make it as easy as they can for customers to use their products. They package products in convenient forms, ensure that instructions are easy to understand, and provide support (via a website or call center) if the customer has questions. In HR, we need to put that same thought, logic, and presentation into helping employees make smart choices—or, *do the right thing*—to take action such as enrolling in benefits by a certain deadline.

For situations where you need employees to take action, make it unbelievably easy for them to do so. Think through where and when they need to act and what prompts will they need. Give them "just in time" prompts to call, log on, or write to get the coverage they should have.

## Protect Your Pay

Here's how Jane responded to the challenge of rolling out a Managed Disability Program. The gist of the program was this: If an employee was out sick or hospitalized for five days or more, she had to call a benefit services representative to get her disability approved. Without this approval, pay would stop.

Many people would have put together the Managed Disability Program communication strategy and plan using sentences like this: "If you don't call while you're out sick or in the hospital, your pay will stop." (Do you talk punitively to your customers? We thought not. It's not a great way to talk with your employees, either.)

Following our mantra of "Make it easy for employees to do the right thing," our communication program centered on a refrigerator magnet mailed to employees at home. The magnet said, "Protect your pay. Call this toll-free number if you're out sick or hospitalized for five days or more so your pay will continue." A small brochure accompanied the magnet, with more program details if an employee wanted to know more. Most employees probably put the magnet on their refrigerator, where it would be handy if needed.

Nowhere in any of the communications was the term Managed Disability Program used. It may be a "term of art" in the world of human resources, but there was no upside to introducing the term to employees—any more than you'd roll out a similarly titled program to customers.

When you start applying "Make it easy for people to do the right thing" to your HR and communication challenges, really think outside the cubicle. Sometimes the best solution might start with changing plan design first and following that up with good communication.

For example, say your goal is to increase enrollment in the company savings plan (or even reach 100% enrollment). One way to achieve that goal is to enroll all employees in the savings plan automatically on Day One, with the provision that they can opt out after six months. Then, if you communicate with employees throughout those six months—pointing out how easy it is to save and sharing projections of how much they can save in both short- and long-term scenarios—perhaps they'll stay in the plan after six months. In this case, you've made inertia (after all, doing nothing really is the easiest thing to do), the right course of "action."

## Checklist for Treating Your Employees as Customers

✓ Create an employee profile that describes a typical employee in key demographic groups.

✓ Include a (fictional) photo in the profiles you create so that you can visualize your employee customer.

✓ Remember this sage advice: "Never underestimate employees' intelligence or overestimate their knowledge."

✓ Use focus groups to assess what employees understand about key policies, programs, and issues.

✓ When surveying or conducting focus groups, include this question: "What is the one thing you would change about how we communicate?"

✓ Give employees the information and tools they need to "do the right thing" when they take action on important programs or policies.

# 3

# Plan and Manage Communication

*In this chapter, you learn how to*

- *Ask great questions to start your communication project effectively*
- *Set clear objectives for your HR communication*
- *Organize and manage communication projects*
- *Establish appropriate budgets*

Let's say you decide to take a trip. Do you begin by jumping in the car, stepping on the gas, pulling onto the highway, and heading west just because the road takes you that way?

Probably not (unless you're 20 years old and setting off on a cross-country road trip to find yourself). Instead, most of us don't depart until we have a clear destination in mind. And once we know where we want to go, we usually plot our course (thanks, Google Maps) or enter the coordinates into our GPS. Since we're busy, we usually choose the shortest route.

Why the travel metaphor? Because it's a good way to illustrate a mistake many of us make in communication: We just start doing it without having a plan or map. How many times have you heard a colleague say, "We need to communicate this program. I'll write an e-mail."? Or "People need to know about this policy. I'll create a PowerPoint presentation."?

If you pull the trigger before taking aim, your communication can miss the mark. Or, you risk using the wrong tool for the wrong job. It can happen too soon, be over too quickly, or not provide what employees need to know to make smart choices. And, to return to our original metaphor, it probably gets lousy gas mileage.

In this chapter, we show you a more efficient way of planning HR communication. Once you put your objectives in place and plan your approach, all the steps to get there become a lot more obvious.

# Start Each Communication Project by Asking Great Questions

Whenever someone says (or you think), "We need to communicate this right away," you should stop, take a deep breath, and ask these two questions:

- Why do we need to communicate this information?
- What do we need employees to know, believe, and/or do as a result?

These are the key foundational questions that will help you set a single overarching goal for your communication as well as develop up to three specific, measurable objectives. We show you how to create goals and objectives in a moment. But in the meantime, as long as you're on a roll, keep asking questions to learn all you can about the need the communication is meant to address. Here are more good questions:

- When do employees need information to take action?
- Does this program support broader company goals?
- How will we know our communications have been successful?
- What obstacles, if any, do we face, and how can we overcome them?

Sometimes people preface their questions by saying, "This is probably a stupid question, but...." And almost always, the response is, "That's a great question." In business, sometimes the best questions are so basic that they almost never get asked. One assumes, instead, and that assumption can lead to miscommunication instead of clear communication.

## Use the Answers to These Questions to Establish a Goal and Objectives

Occasionally you need to take some time to ask questions about what you want to achieve and how you know if you're successful before you arrive at

- Your overarching goal
- Your objectives (in most cases, aim for up to three objectives)
- How you'll measure your success in achieving your objectives

The process of asking questions and then establishing your goal and objectives will keep you from developing objectives that are unrealistic, unreasonable, or unachievable.

For example, if a colleague wants to "make employees feel good about the fact that we're not paying any bonuses this year," you'll have a hard time achieving that objective. It's unrealistic, and it's also highly unlikely that people will feel good about not receiving money they were probably counting on.

Suppose you change the preceding objective to "Help employees understand why we can't pay bonuses this year—and share three steps we can all take to improve the chances we'll receive bonuses next year." You have a better chance of achieving that objective, because it is realistic, and you can measure it. For example, you could conduct a random online survey after you communicate.

One of the simplest ways to see if you've set clear objectives for your communication is to determine how you'll measure success. If you can't figure out how to measure the success of your objectives, try restating the objective until you can come up with a way to measure whether you've achieved it.

## What's the Difference Between a Goal and an Objective?

Many dictionaries have similar definitions for "goal" and "objective":

**Goal**: A broad statement of what you hope to accomplish. May suggest an idealistic or long-term purpose.

**Objective**: Often implies that the end or goal can be reached.

Here's a useful overview for project management purposes:

| Goal | Objective |
|---|---|
| Broad overview of what we want to do over time | Specifically what we want to accomplish soon |
| The purpose of our actions | What we want to accomplish |
| Long term | Short term |
| Not easily measured | Can be measured |

## Questioning Helps Identify Personal Agendas, Too

When you start a communication project, ask yourself (or your client) if there's anything you *personally* want to accomplish while working on this project. For example, do you have a personal developmental goal you want to achieve? A specific experience you'd like to have? What would make this project a winner for you? Invest some time in thinking about what you want to achieve or experience. Your personal goal could be "Build better relationships with my peers in the Marketing department" or "Learn how to give a better presentation" or "Get some visibility at headquarters."

The Center for Creative Leadership is an educational organization that teaches leaders to be more effective. It has determined through research that we learn most of the information that helps us succeed through on-the-job experiences—not from seminars or training courses. Therefore, it's important to determine what you can personally achieve—or what your client can personally achieve—while you help your company or HR department reach a specific goal.

## Is It an E-mail or a Video? Or Is It Another Solution Desperately Seeking a Problem to Solve?

A colleague once enthusiastically approached us and said, "We need to produce a video about this conference I just hosted! I'd like to begin working on it right away!" Ten minutes into our conversation, after we'd asked the colleague a lot of questions, we realized that a video was not a good idea.

What were our colleague's objectives? To inform the HR community about the highlights of the conference in an easy-to-digest way.

Although video *can* be effective, "highlights" videos of conferences tend to be dull shots of people presenting (with equally dull PowerPoint to match). Even footage of interactive segments (such as team-building exercises) tends to seem out of context. Plus, the audience might view video highlights as follows: "Oh, look, Marge. All the really important people went off to this fancy resort, and even though I wasn't important enough to be invited, I did receive this long video with a bunch of talking heads."

After discussing our colleague's objectives, we suggested a different idea: "Perhaps we can help you write an e-mail about this," with links to intranet content. We also advised our colleague to send conference attendees an e-mail with key points (such as action steps) that they could share with their staffs and colleagues in other departments.

*continued*

If you want conference participants to "bring the conference home," it is a good idea to establish that as one of your objectives while you're still planning the conference. This way, you can let attendees know that's a goal, and you can make it easy for participants to do the right thing and share what they learned.

# Manage HR Communication Projects Effectively

Huge tomes exist that tell you in great detail how to manage a communication project effectively. In some cases, reading that tome might be a great investment of your time and talent. Here, we share some faster, simpler ways to help you get your work done.

Here's one of the simplest project plans for any HR communication, presented in just four easy steps:

1. Research
2. Plan
3. Do
4. Measure

If you have one hour—or one week—to get something done, this is a great way to organize your time. For example, suppose your boss or client needs information in one hour for an e-mail to all employees to announce a new fund in the company's 401(k) plan. Also assume that e-mail is the best and only vehicle to communicate that employees should take advantage of the opportunity to invest immediately. You'd want to spend the first part of that hour asking questions or doing online research to learn more about the purpose of the new fund, who should be investing in it, why, and so on.

What you learn will help you plan—that is, help you decide how you want to present this information given your employee demographics. It will dictate the types of examples you present. If you spent 20 minutes doing research and planning, now spend 25 minutes writing your e-mail and editing it to keep it as brief as possible. Make sure that the subject line and boldface subheads help your readers skim and get valuable information. Finally, share your finished product with a colleague to measure whether your communication works. Does your colleague understand what you want every reader to understand? If not, make some tweaks so it's crystal clear. Then take your e-mail to your boss or client to review.

The following sections discuss more activities you can consider doing in each of these simple steps.

## *Research*

- Get the demographic, geographic, and psychographic information about your audience.
- Identify what communications (media and messages) have worked well with this audience in the past—or what media and messages would logically work well with this audience at this time.
- List any obstacles or misunderstandings you need to address in your communication.
- Find out what your competitors have done in similar circumstances, if applicable.
- Find out what companies your management admires have done in similar circumstances.

If you have a board of directors, find out what your board members' companies have done in similar circumstances. Just spending an hour or so using Google should give you a lot of useful information. Government or industry statistics can help you put information in context, for example. The research phase can take weeks, days, or merely hours or minutes. However long it lasts, make sure you spend some time on research and fact-gathering. All the great work you do in planning and implementing can't make up for shoddy research.

## Plan

- Make decisions about media, messages, and process based on your research. Test your plans with a sampling of your eventual audiences and also with all key stakeholders (other departments you need to coordinate with so that your project goes smoothly).
- Revise your plans based on what you learn.

This is the time to invite your colleagues to help make your work better (and get them invested in your project's success, too). As one of our colleagues wisely said, "Share your good work, and let others share in its success." We agree.

## Do

In this step, you create and distribute your communication which includes writing copy, videotaping, designing print and presentation materials, getting stuff printed—all the usual things you need to do to get your message presented, packaged, and distributed. (We cover this step in a lot more detail throughout this book.)

## Measure

In Chapter 9, "Measure Effectiveness," we provide a comprehensive view of effective communication measurement. But keep these steps in mind as you plan:

- Include a survey in written or electronic communications.
- Share what you learn from measuring success with your management and colleagues.

## So, How Long Will This Take?

Possibly one of the most frequently asked questions about communication projects is some variation of "How fast can you get this done?"

With an unlimited budget, you can move mountains and get communications produced quickly by working overtime. With a less ambitious budget, experience shows you can produce good work anywhere between three weeks and three months. It depends on the topic, its complexity, and the need for multiple shareholders to agree, to name just a few variables. One of our favorite graphic designers used to quip, "If you want it fast, cheap, and high quality, pick any two." We agree. Taking the time to do research and to test communications with focus groups is literally priceless in the value they provide. You'll never regret an investment in time that helps you create effective communications.

# Create Award-Winning Communications and Communication Plans

When Jane facilitated a two-day conference for communication managers in Houston, she invited Otto Glade, a local communication professional, to speak to the group. He had won numerous Gold Quill awards of excellence from the International Association of Business Communicators (IABC), a worldwide professional organization for organizational communicators. Jane asked him to share his secrets for success with the group.

Otto's formula was simple and elegant: He used the IABC Gold Quill entry form as a project plan for each communication he produced. This helped him stay focused on what information he needed to do a good job. This strategy can work the same way for you.

If you use this structure to describe your communication plan, you'll typically end up with a two- to three-page project overview. This is a great way to sell your idea to colleagues and management in your company or client's company.

Here's an overview of what the Gold Quill award entry form typically asks you to describe:

- **Need/opportunity.** What need or opportunity does your communication project address? Clearly describe the issues your company faces, and outline any effect these issues have on

company performance, reputation, image, profits, and participation. Highlight any formal or informal research findings that
support your analysis of the need or opportunity.

- **Intended audience(s).** Identify your primary audience and
any other audiences. What is your audience's state of mind?
What key audience characteristics do you need to take into
account as you develop your solution? Consider psychographic
as well as demographic characteristics. Describe any audience
research you plan to conduct.

- **Goals and objectives.** Goals describe what your communication project is designed to accomplish. Choose one or two key
goals to describe in detail. These goals should be aligned with
your organization's future needs. Objectives should be realistic
and measurable and should examine outcomes such as quantity, quality, time, cost, percentages, or other criteria. These
measures are often financial, but not always.

- **Solution overview.** Outline your project's solution and the
logic that supports it. Describe why you plan to take the action
you've outlined. The solution should demonstrate your thought
process, imagination, and approach to problem solving. Discuss
how you will involve stakeholders in developing the solution.
Identify key messages. Present the tactics and communication
vehicles you plan to use. Identify your role in the project and
your level of involvement and responsibility.

- **Implementation and challenges.** State your project budget.
Show how you plan to make efficient use of money. Discuss
time frames. Describe any limitations or challenges that you
face as you communicate and implement your ideas. Note any
special circumstances, and discuss how they will be addressed.

- **Measurement/evaluation of outcomes.** How will you
measure your project's results? Every result should be linked
to one or more objectives. Results must be shown to be valuable, thorough, and convincing. Measurement should demonstrate outcomes, not outputs. For example, if your media
relations campaign was designed to support a product rollout,
you should measure bottom-line figures about sales targets or
the number of qualified sales leads, rather than just measuring

the number of clips and impressions or advertising value equivalent. If your challenge was to improve employees' understanding of an issue, you must show that their knowledge increased as a result of the communication plan you implemented.

# Describe Your Communication Project Succinctly

The best way to describe your communication project in the fewest possible words is to identify the following elements and then put them into a single sentence:

- Who
- What
- When
- Where
- Why
- How

Here's how that would work for several different projects:

| Topic | Project One | Project Two | Project Three |
|---|---|---|---|
| **Who** (subject) | Financial experts | All company managers | Health and safety officials |
| **What** (action verb) | Provide advice to all employees | Work with employees to identify and put new steps into practice | Encourage workers to follow new safety procedures |
| **When** | Throughout this year | Each fiscal quarter | This month |
| **Where** | At headquarters | Nationally | In all factories |
| **Why** | To cut expenses | To increase profits | To reduce accidents |
| **How** | Seminars, website, and how-to kits | Informational campaign via e-mail, website, print, and meeting-in-a-box kits | Posters, mailings to home, meetings, and $100 for each worker if objectives are reached |

Newspaper reporters use this technique to write the lead sentence in any news article—just identify the who, what, when, where, why, and how (the last two being the hardest to determine in some cases—especially crime stories).

Here's a one-sentence overview of each of these projects:

- **Project One.** To help us cut expenses here at company headquarters, throughout the year financial experts will share advice with employees in special seminars, on our website, and in how-to kits.
- **Project Two.** To increase profits, a new quarterly informational campaign, including meeting-in-a-box kits, e-mails, website, and printed instructions, will provide all company managers with information they need to work with their staffs to identify and put into practice steps to help us reach our goal.
- **Project Three.** Bet you can tackle this one on your own.

# Establish an Appropriate Budget

Jane once heard an HR director proudly announce, "Now that our intranet is up, we'll never have to produce another brochure or newsletter for employees. We can save all that money and stop killing trees!"

## The Truth About Killing Trees

As a small aside, paper companies raise trees like any other crop these days (and no one is crying about killing corn!). Trees are planted, harvested, and replenished, just like corn. Recycled paper has grown as an industry and offers another good option, albeit a more expensive one. Please share this information with the next person who tells you that producing print means "killing trees."

Let's think for a minute about the wisdom of eliminating print. It's like saying now that we have e-mail, we'll never need to send our customers another brochure. Maybe not. Yet, in our experience, sometimes print does the best job for your employees, so we encourage you not to limit yourself to electronic communication tools. In Chapter 7, "Use the Right Tool for the Job," we talk about using the right tool for the right job, and you'll see that print still performs a valuable service.

Now, back to budgeting. Here are several ways to determine budgets for HR communications projects:

- **Unit cost.** Come up with a "per employee" cost to inform each employee of a specific benefit (or determine the unit cost to communicate *all* HR benefits and services). The more employees who work at your company, the lower your unit cost will be. Compare the unit cost of *communicating* to the actual cost of *providing* all benefits/one benefit to an employee. Obviously, your unit cost to communicate should be a small percentage of the much larger cost to provide the benefit.

- **Percentage of salary cost.** Determine how much money your company spends on payroll, and then develop a communication budget for the year based on a percentage of your organization's salary cost. Ideally, your communication budget won't exceed 10% of the cost of pay.

  Whatever amount you propose to spend on communicating, you can make the case that you're spending an amount equal to X% of the cost of all employees to make sure they understand, use, and value HR products and services.

- **Percentage of benefit cost.** If it costs your company $200,000 a year to provide a specific benefit, isn't it worth up to $20,000—or up to 10% of the benefit's cost—to make sure everyone understands, uses, and values that benefit? Again, you can use this logic to build a budget for one specific benefit or all benefits as a group.

You may also want to look at the money your company spends on advertising and marketing—and then develop your HR communication budget as a derivative of the dollars spent in those areas. Some of the communications you produce are *legally required*, you could also see what your company's annual legal budget is and propose your annual HR communications budget as a derivative of that number.

Depending on your industry, and your company's ability to attract and keep needed talent, you may also want to find out what your competitors are spending on HR communications. This information might not be as useful as what we just discussed in helping you develop a budget. But it could help you make your case even more solid when you present your budget to management.

Basically, we're suggesting that you base your budget for communications on a derivative of numbers familiar to your management team. Also propose funding that makes sense for your company's size, competition, and revenues.

# And When There Is No Money . . . Sigh

If you work for a not-for-profit organization, or for a company that only a Scrooge would love (and who among us has not?), some of the preceding suggestions might work for you. Yet you may find that you rarely have the budget dollars to do the quality of work you want—the level of quality that will promote effective use of HR benefits and services.

Here are some further ideas to help you supplement a weak budget:

- Get employees involved as photographers or illustrators for your HR communication materials.
- Invite a local graphic arts instructor to present his or her students with your communication needs as an assignment.
- Ask a donor (contributor) company to provide the resources of its HR communication team to help your HR communication team.

# Checklist to Manage Your Communication Project Effectively

✓ Decide what you want your employees to know—to understand—or do at the start of each HR communication project.

✓ Clarify your goal and up to three objectives for your project. Specify how you'll measure success for each objective you set.

✓ Identify what you want to get out of the project on a personal level (such as what developmental experience you want to have).

✓ Create a simple project plan to help organize and manage your project.

✓ Invest in the time needed to do research up front and to get feedback on complex communications through focus group tests.

✓ Develop a budget for your project that appropriately reflects the importance of the message and the importance of your objectives.

✓ Summarize what you're doing by identifying the who, what, when, where, why, and how. Then express the results in a single sentence or paragraph.

# 4

# Frame Your Message

*In this chapter, you learn*

- *How to "frame" your message: organize it in a way that meets employees' needs and helps them understand how the pieces fit*
- *Why the way you communicate with employees needs to be different from how you pitch programs to management*
- *How to leverage techniques from Hollywood to distill your message*
- *What the old-fashioned telegram can teach us about structuring content*
- *How to use a mathematical formula—1-3-9-27—to organize communication*

You've just given a presentation to senior management about your new program. Your PowerPoint deck was appropriately detailed: 44 slides explaining why the program is needed, how you designed it, and what it contains. And your hard work paid off, because the meeting went well; management approved the program, giving you the go-ahead to implement it.

Now it's time to communicate with employees. And here's the first thing you should do: Close the PowerPoint file and take out a blank sheet of paper. Why? Because the way you structured your message to "sell" your program to management is very different from how you need to frame your message for your employee audience.

Again, why? As you saw in Chapter 2, "Treat Your Employees Like Customers," it starts with demographics: Your employee audience has a different perspective than senior managers. And that difference means you need to rethink how you shape your key messages to meet the needs of your employee audience.

*How the Communication Needs of Senior Managers and Employees Differ*

|  | Senior Managers | Employees |
|---|---|---|
| **Most important part of the message** | Context: How this helps the company succeed | Personal impact: "What this means to me" and "What I need to do differently" |
| **Level of detail** | High: To demonstrate that all aspects of the issue were thoroughly explored | Low: Quickly get to the point |
| **Preferred channel** | Presentation with discussion | Varies by group: some written, some spoken, some visual |
| **Tools** | Charts, graphs, analyses | Key points, bullets, checklists |
| **Time spent** | Several hours | Several minutes |

So how do you proceed? Here's the essence: Refer to the objectives you created in Chapter 3, "Plan and Manage Communication." With those objectives in mind, use that blank piece of paper to answer this question: What's the most important thing employees need to know? As you write the answer, limit your response to 15 words or less.

Congratulations! You've just "framed" your message: You've created a core statement that captures the essence of what you need to communicate. You've also created the foundation for a message platform, which will help you organize all your communication about your new program.

This sounds good, but if this task is new to you, you may need some help. Stay with us; we show you three easy-to-use approaches to framing your message:

- "Go Hollywood" to create a high concept
- Use the inverted pyramid to organize your message
- Leverage the 3-9-27 formula to structure content

# "Go Hollywood" to Create a High Concept

We know what you're thinking: What does Hollywood have to do with HR communication? Well, as you've probably figured out by now, we believe in borrowing the best techniques from any field to make our communication more effective.

And, as it turns out, no one is better than Hollywood's movie studios at distilling a product into just a few words and at making that message riveting to audiences around the world. Movie promoters have realized that they have just a few seconds to capture an audience's attention as people walk by a movie poster or flip through TV channels. So movie people have figured out how to capture the essence of a film in a single, simple statement.

That statement, in movie talk, is called a "high concept." The idea is that, in order to pitch (to a producer or the audience), you have to convey an entire two-hour movie in about 12 to 15 words. Once the movie gets the green light, the high concept is used as the basis of all marketing, including ads, posters, publicity, e-mails, and websites.

### Going Up!

Here's another term for "high concept": an "elevator speech." The idea is that you get into an elevator with a colleague who says something like, "Hey, I hear we're changing the vacation policy. What's up with that?" Your challenge is to answer the question in the time it takes to ride the elevator; that's why it's called an elevator speech.

By the way, the latest term for delivering information quickly and concisely is an "escalator speech." The assumption is that you don't even have as much time as it takes to ride the elevator: You have only about 20 seconds, or the length of time it takes to say about 140 characters (the standard length of a "tweet" on the social media platform Twitter or a status update on LinkedIn or Facebook).

## And the Oscar Goes to . . .

Based on the following "high-concept" statements, name the Academy Award-winning movie:*

a. A teenager is one question away from winning India's "Who Wants to Be a Millionaire." But is he cheating?

b. A selfish man seeking his inheritance discovers his autistic savant brother, abducts him, and takes him on a cross-country road trip.

c. A rich girl and a poor boy meet on the ill-fated voyage of the "unsinkable" ship.

d. In 1930s Austria, a woman leaves a convent to become a governess to a Naval officer widower with seven children.

Here's why we love the "high concept": because you can use the technique to communicate anything—a new initiative, changes to a benefits program, a company strategy. The key is to boil down a complicated idea into its essence so that your audience can understand it instantly.

---

* Answers: a) *Slumdog Millionaire*, b) *Rainman*, c) *Titanic*, d) *The Sound of Music*

## Long-Term Disability Gets the "High Concept" Treatment

Sheila, the compensation and benefits director at a major pharmaceutical company, faced a challenge: Not enough employees were signing up for the company's long-term disability program. Sheila knew that one in five U.S. workers suffer an accident or illness that prevents them from working for months at a time. And she also knew that many of her company's employees did not have the savings to weather a long period without pay. So how could she persuade more employees to enroll in the company program?

First, Sheila worked with her company's provider to make changes to the disability program that would make it more appealing to employees. Once senior management approved the changes, Sheila took our advice and put away the PowerPoint she had used at the management meeting. Instead, she took out a blank piece of paper.

Her mission: to write a "high concept" of about 12 to 15 words that would convey the benefits of the new long-term disability plan. After some deliberation, Sheila wrote the following:

*Long-Term Disability Plan gives you more coverage for less money*

Not bad. But we'd suggest that Sheila also try to include why long-term disability is so important. Here's what we mean:

*Protect your income if you can't work; new Long-Term Disability Plan offers more coverage for less money*

You get the idea. The key is to capture your main point succinctly. It takes some finesse to balance the need to be brief with the need to include enough information. But the more you practice the high-concept approach, the more confident you will become.

## High-Concept Worksheet

Here's an opportunity to practice your new knowledge of creating the high concept. We've completed the first one; it's up to you to create a high concept for the others.

| Issue You Need to Communicate | High-Concept Summary (15 Words or Less) |
| --- | --- |
| In addition to the company-paid life insurance plan, which automatically provides coverage equal to an employee's annual salary, the company now offers a voluntary group life insurance plan. This gives employees the opportunity to purchase additional life insurance at group rates, which are cheaper than what employees would pay with individual policies. | Through the company group life insurance plan, you can buy additional coverage at cheaper rates. |
| Next year, your company will switch dental plan providers from Guardian to MetLife PPO. The change is being made to reduce plan costs to the company. MetLife has more in-network dentists than Guardian. A slight increase (less than 3%) in employee premiums will occur. The deductible will increase from $25 to $50. The annual maximum coverage will increase from $2,000 to $2,500 (a positive change for employees). Orthodontic coverage will not change. | |
| The tuition reimbursement process is changing. In the past, employees wanting to get approval for a course had to fill out a paper form, get their supervisor to sign it, and send it to HR. Now employees need to visit the HR portal, fill out an electronic form, and ask their supervisors to access the form to complete their section. The amount of tuition reimbursement isn't changing. | |

# Use the Inverted Pyramid to Organize Your Message

Now that you've got the essence of your message, what do you do next? We suggest you turn back the clock to an antiquated form of communication—the telegram—for inspiration on how to organize your content.

Back in the 19th century, newspaper reporters relied on the telegram to send a breaking news item to their editors. The problem was that, especially in the early days, the telegram was unreliable; the lines were always going down for one reason or another, such as high winds or Indian attacks.

So reporters began structuring their messages with the most important news first, in descending order of importance to the end. That way, if only part of the telegram got through before the transmission was interrupted, the newspapers would still get the scoop.

Around this time, editors began to encourage all their reporters to use this structure, whether or not they had to use a telegraph. "Write 15 inches of copy on that story," an editor would tell a reporter. The story would be typeset, and if the editor didn't have room for the entire story, it would be easy to him to cut from the bottom to fit the space available.

This way of organizing information came to be known as the inverted pyramid. The top contains the most critical points, and the bottom contains details or optional information, as shown in Figure 4-1.

Way back in the day, when Jane was in journalism school, budding reporters learned another technique to help them create the first paragraph of the pyramid: five Ws and an H. She learned that the lead paragraph of a news story is the most that many readers will read or scan, so she was urged to make sure to convey the following elements to communicate the most important information:

- **Who:** The subject of your communication
- **What:** The action: what action will occur, what needs to happen
- **When:** The date the change will occur
- **Where:** The location(s)
- **Why:** The motivation behind or reason for the action
- **How:** The process and method of the action

Fast-forward to today's fast-paced, information-overloaded world. You may be surprised to learn that the old-fashioned inverted pyramid is still the best format for much of the information you need to convey. Employees are too busy to sit and read content from start to finish; they want to skim and scan to get to the most relevant parts. So the inverted pyramid provides a quick, easy-to-digest way to get information.

Remember that the same principle you used to develop your high concept applies to the inverted pyramid: The information most important to employees comes first. As you travel down the pyramid, you can then add context and details.

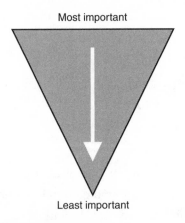

Figure 4-1   The inverted pyramid

### *"Am I Doing This Wrong?"*

After Alison gave a presentation on best practices in communication at a regional HR conference in DeKalb, Illinois, she opened the floor to questions. A woman in the front row raised her hand.

"I'm an HR manager for a hospital," she said by way of introduction. "You said that the most effective way to create a message is to put the most important, most relevant information up front."

"That's right," said Alison.

"Early in my career, I was taught that you tell the story in chronological order. So when I send an e-mail to employees about a benefits change, for example, I start with why we decided to make a change and what options we explored. And then I write about what's changing." She paused. "Am I doing this wrong?"

Alison hesitated. She didn't want to insult the HR manager, but she had to tell her the truth.

"Sorry, but yes, you are," Alison said. "What employees need first is what's changing and what the change means to them. They may want the background information eventually, but make sure it comes much further down in the message."

#### An Inverted Pyramid for Long-Term Disability

Remember Sheila and her new Long-Term Disability Plan? After she drafted her high concept, Sheila wrote an e-mail about the plan. She put the most important information first, then organized the content in descending order, with details at the end. Here's what she wrote:

**Protect your income with the new Long-Term Disability Plan**

**Provides more coverage for less money**

*Sign up during Open Enrollment*

What would happen to you and your family if you couldn't work for an extended time because of a serious injury or illness? Because most people don't have enough savings to cover expenses, a long-term disability (one lasting more than 26 weeks) often puts them in financial jeopardy. But you can protect yourself by signing up for the Company's Long-Term Disability (LTD) Plan. And this is a great year to do so, because the plan has been modified to cost less and provide greater coverage.

Disability insurance pays a portion of your salary if you become unable to work due to an illness or injury unrelated to your job. (Workers' Compensation covers job-related injuries.) For the first 26 weeks you are out of work, you are automatically covered by the Company's Basic Short-Term Disability Plan. After 26 weeks, you need the Long-Term Plan, which covers you as long as you are disabled, or until age 65.

This year's Open Enrollment is a great time to enroll in LTD. That's because the Company has redesigned the program to include the following:

- **Lower contributions.** The Company has negotiated better rates, so the cost for LTD next year will be nearly 50% lower than last year.

- **One-time waiver for evidence of good health.** For coverage next year only, you can enroll in LTD without a medical screening. (If you don't enroll now, but you want to do so later, a medical screening will be required.)

- **Increase to full coverage for current enrollees.** If you are currently enrolled in LTD at a maximum coverage of $5,000 (because you either did not submit evidence of good health or were declined a higher amount of coverage), your benefits will be increased automatically to the full benefit amount.

To find out more, visit the HR portal or call the HR service center at XXX-XXX-XXXX.

# Leverage the 1-3-9-27 Formula to Structure Content

Math may not have been your favorite subject in school, but when it comes to structuring complex content, a simple mathematical model can be your friend. That model is 1-3-9-27. This doesn't stand for a multiplication equation; it represents a format you can use to organize even the most detailed communication.

Here's what it looks like:

| 1 High Concept | | | |
|---|---|---|---|
| 3 Key Messages | | | |
| 9 Supporting Points | point | point | point |
| | point | point | point |
| | point | point | point |
| 27 Details | detail | detail | detail |
| | detail | detail | detail |
| | detail | detail | detail |
| | detail | detail | detail |
| | detail | detail | detail |
| | detail | detail | detail |
| | detail | detail | detail |
| | detail | detail | detail |
| | detail | detail | detail |

This principle is the same as the one used to organize a closet. When your content is arranged by category (shoes, handbags, dresses), it's easier to store, view, and find when you need it. Especially when you're dealing with detailed issues such as health and retirement plans, 1-3-9-27 puts everything in its place—which helps employees easily understand the content when you communicate.

Plus, 1-3-9-27 builds on the foundation we've described throughout this chapter: You start with your high concept, develop key messages (the same as you would for building an inverted pyramid), and then fill in the details.

Depending on the topic, you may not use all the elements of 1-3-9-27, but you know the structure is there if you need it.

## Filling in the Blanks

Sheila found the form helpful for plotting the details of changes to her Long-Term Disability Plan. You may notice that she has structured her content slightly differently than when she wrote the e-mail using the inverted pyramid. That's because this time she tried to organize all the related content, not just emphasize the advantages of the new plan.

Although Sheila thought the 1-3-9-27 table was useful, she realized that she didn't need to fill in all the blanks, because her plan doesn't have a lot of details. (But she thought 1-3-9-27 might really come in handy when communicating open enrollment.)

| 1 High Concept | Protect your income if you can't work; new Long-Term Disability Plan offers more coverage for less money | | |
|---|---|---|---|
| 3 Key Messages | Lower contributions: Employee cost for LTD will be nearly 50% lower than last year. | Better coverage | Other changes employees need to know |

| 9 Supporting Points | Reduced contributions begin on Jan. 1. Your monthly cost is based on a formula derived from a percentage of your income. Example: Chris, a 33-year-old employee, has an annual salary of $50,000. He is currently paying $19.75 a month for LTD. Next year, he will pay only $9.49, a savings of $10.26 a month. | One-time waiver for evidence of good health: For coverage this year only, you can enroll in LTD without a medical screening. No exclusions for preexisting conditions. Increase to full coverage amount for current enrollees. | Disability benefits will not be paid from the retirement plan for individuals who become disabled after December 31. Beginning January 1, Medicare Part B premiums will no longer be paid for disabled people who qualify for Medicare. |
| --- | --- | --- | --- |
| 27 Details | For employees who qualify, a pension supplement is paid beginning at age 65. | | |

# Checklist for Framing Your Message

✓ Start with your objectives: What do you need employees to believe and do? That becomes the foundation of your message.

✓ Put away the PowerPoint you used to present to senior management, and start with a clean sheet of paper. Remember that what matters most to leaders may be quite different from what employees want to learn.

✓ Steal a technique from Hollywood and create a "high concept": a single statement (of 15 words or less) that captures the key message you want to convey.

✓ Create your content using an old-fashioned journalism framework called the inverted pyramid. Put the most important
information first, and then arrange the remaining information
in order of descending importance, down to the details.

✓ Try the 1-3-9-27 method for organizing all your details, especially for more complicated communications.

# 5

# Write Simply and Clearly

*In this chapter, you learn how to*

- *Attract readers the same way magazines, newspapers, and advertisers do*
- *Package information in memorable, easy-to-read chunks*
- *Write in a way that everyone will understand*
- *Use stories, specific examples, and concrete language*
- *Check your writing one last time to make sure it's good to go*

You're waiting in the airport when you hear the bad news over the PA system: Your departure has been delayed for two hours. So, with time to kill, you head to the newsstand and browse the magazine racks. Here's some good news: Those magazines are not just entertainment; they're also inspiration for how to write HR content simply and clearly. The same techniques that editors use to get you to read their magazines, advertisers also use to encourage you to buy their products and newspapers use to inform you—all work equally well in the world of HR communication.

That's because effective writing follows universal principles. Employees do not differentiate how they react to communications at work versus at home. They don't say, "This isn't easy to understand, but that's okay, because it's just from my company." They don't say, "The company video with those talking heads was boring, but I watched it anyway," because they wouldn't watch a boring movie at home. They wouldn't read a long, rambling, complex article online or in print, and they won't do that at work either.

# Earn Points for Doing It Well

When you write in short, easy-to-read, conversational language that everyone can understand, *everyone will*. We show you how, in five simple steps:

1. Convey what matters most to employees.
2. Emphasize "how to."
3. Slice, dice, and chunk content.
4. Use plain language.
5. Be concrete.

### *Convey What Matters Most to Employees*

In Chapter 4, "Frame Your Message," we showed you how to develop a "high concept" to summarize your key message, and how to use the inverted pyramid to organize your message. We also shared an important reporters' tool—five Ws and an H, which is used in journalism to convey essential facts. We think the five Ws and an H are so integral to successful writing that we're showing them to you again:

- **Who:**   The subject of your communication
- **What:**   The action: what action will occur, what needs to happen
- **When:**   The date the change will occur
- **Where:**   The location(s)
- **Why:**   The motivation behind or reason for the action
- **How:**   The process and method of the action

Here's the key: As you capture the five Ws and an H, focus on the employee. Ask and answer these questions from the employee's point of view:

- What does this mean to me?
- Why is this important?
- What do I need to do?
- When do I need to act?

Put that important information up front in your communication, and then reinforce this information throughout: in photo captions, subheads, callout quotes, stories, tables, and charts.

## A Few Good Ws (and an H)

Sometimes the five Ws and an H are so useful that an entire communication piece can be constructed around them. Here's a case in point. A biotechnology company needed to let employees know about a pay change. The company operated on a fiscal year, and it was changing to align its pay raises with the performance management cycle. To communicate the change, the company created a one-page piece. Here are the highlights:

**Company Changes Pay Cycle; Raise Schedule Affected**

**What is changing**

- The pay cycle: when and how salary raises are paid. Starting this year, pay raises will become effective on September 1 instead of in July.

**What is *not* changing**

- The performance management schedule, which still runs from July 1 to June 30
- The performance management system

**Why the change?**

- To improve efficiency. Payroll systems are being consolidated across the company, so we're moving to a consistent schedule.
- To create a better performance/pay system. This change allows us to roll out future improvements—such as online performance and compensation tools—more easily across the company.

*continued*

**How will you be affected?**

*This year:*

- Your raise will become effective on September 1, and you'll see the increase in your first September pay.

- If you received a retroactive payment in September for July/August raises, that will end with this year's pay adjustment.

- The move from July to September will be factored into the salary budget provided to each manager.

*Next year:*

- Your raise will become effective on September 1.

**What do you need to do?**

- Understand the pay cycle change. Get the details by visiting [the HR portal].

- Get more information if you need it by calling XXX-XXX-XXXX.


*Emphasize "How To"*

Remember that scene in the airport newsstand when your flight was delayed and you were looking at magazines? If you meandered over to the section with consumer magazines—such as *Good Housekeeping, Men's Health, Better Homes and Gardens, Bon Appetit,* and *Seventeen*—you might have noticed something about the "cover lines" (the short headlines that promote what's inside that issue). Here's a sampling of what you might have seen:

- How one "Biggest Loser" *really* lost 140 pounds
- Banish beauty blunders
- Drop a dress size in 6 weeks
- Make dinner like a pro—in just 30 minutes
- 7 success strategies your CEO doesn't want you to know

- Sleep deeply | Wake up energized
- How to love a crazy job
- Your best spring garden ever

What do these cover lines have in common? They promise to help readers solve a problem, improve something they do, and, fundamentally, be happier. Magazine editors use these lines because they know that "you" and "how to" are the most compelling headline words you can use. They're so compelling, in fact, that they work even if you don't explicitly use them. ("Sleep deeply" is short for "Here's how you can sleep deeply." We get that "you" and "how to" are implied.)

The official name for this approach is "service journalism," explains Don Ranly, professor emeritus at the University of Missouri School of Journalism. We often quote Dr. Ranly because he has such good advice about how to present information. The idea behind service journalism is that you (the writer) perform a **service** for the reader by putting together useful "how to" information. In other words, if you package information in a way that is *useful* for readers, they will be more likely to *use* that information to take action.

(Don also calls this technique "refrigerator journalism" because people cut out or print useful articles and post them where they will see them every day—on the refrigerator door.)

In short, the secret that advertisers and magazine editors know is that people crave information that makes things easier, simpler, faster, and better. So if you write your messages that way, employees will pay attention.

### Write "Benefit" Headlines Like Advertisers Do

Advertisers know that the most successful headlines are what they call "benefit" heads: headlines that tell you what benefits their products offer you, such as give you softer skin or whiter teeth. (Smart advertisers don't emphasize a product's "features," such as the number of servings or list of ingredients, because customers don't find those as appealing.)

While HR programs rarely give employees softer skin, most HR "products" do offer employees tangible benefits. So your headlines should focus on those benefits, not list the features.

For example, a *feature* of your retirement plan may be that it offers employees eight different investment funds. A *benefit* of your retirement plan may be that the company matches employee contributions dollar for dollar. Which will appeal most to employees? Here are two headlines. Which do you think most employees will be drawn to?

- "Our retirement plan offers you eight different investment options"
- "How you can be paid to save" or "How to double your savings"

### Tell Readers "How To"

Luckily, HR information lends itself to service journalism because it personally affects employees, and there's often a how-to component.

Here are some examples of how to follow Don's advice to create headlines that provide a service for your employees. (All would engage employees' interest much more than a bland heading like "Your Medical Plan.")

- Money (subhead: How you can make more of it and save for tomorrow)
- How to make sound investment decisions
- How to decide what amount of life insurance you need
- 5 ways to increase your productivity without leaving your workstation
- How flexible work arrangements create a win-win for you and your employer
- 3 steps to choose your best medical coverage

## *Use Odd Numbers for Maximum Retention*

A noted writer with lots of experience in the business press once confided this wonderful little secret to us: Odd numbers are more memorable than even numbers. That's why you'll find lots of "3 ways to..." and "5 things to remember..." and "7 ways to solve a problem" in our collected works.

## *Slice, Dice, and Chunk Content*

No, we won't give you a cooking lesson or try to sell you one of those infomercial products ("It slices! It dices! It does your laundry!"). Instead, we show you how to cut your copy into manageable chunks so that employees quickly get your message.

*The bad news you know already:*

**People do not read!**

The next time someone wants to communicate complicated information in great detail, remind him or her of the following facts:

- Most people read only headlines and the first paragraphs.
- People are likely to stop reading if materials include words they don't understand.
- Most employees spend less than one minute reading a newsletter.
- It takes an average reader one minute to read 200 words.
- Web readers read 25% slower and scan 79% of the time, reading only 20% to 28% of the words. Only 16% read word for word.

We need to "chunk" because we've become a society of skimmers and scanners, glancing through a print publication or browsing in a website to find what we need quickly. We read shorter chunks of information more readily than we will read huge, gray columns of words with no break in sight.

As a result, communicators need to find ways to package our content into "chunks" that make it easy for our audience to dive in and remember information.

For example, you'll notice that we liberally use bullet points throughout this book. That's because bullets help you do the following:

- Present an easy-to-scan list of words
- Give readers a series of instructions
- Divide a long, complex sentence into discrete select points

We just showed you an example of what happens if you take a long sentence and divide it so that each bullet starts with a verb. That's another hidden benefit of bullets: They beg for parallel construction that creates a nice, easy rhythm for the reader. We prefer to use verbs as the starting point for bullets because verbs communicate action.

Of course, bullets aren't the only way to chunk your content. You can also try the following:

| Chunking Method | When to Use It |
| --- | --- |
| Checklist | Another form of bulleted list, but the checklist creates an expectation of action, as in a to-do list |
| Numbered sequence | Indicates that there are a certain number of points or action steps to pay attention to |
| Sidebar | Content relating to the main topic that adds context or provides further texture |
| Callout | A short piece of information, such as a quote or single fact |
| Table | A great way to organize complex information. (Originally, we wanted to present this information in a bulleted list, until we realized that a table is easier to read and better organized.) |

## Create a Checklist to Guide Employees Through a Process

It was open enrollment time, and our client, a benefits manager for a large corporation, had a lot to communicate. So we helped her create an enrollment package that used every chunking tool available, including this overview:

**Open Enrollment Checklist**

1. Review and compare each benefit plan option.
   - ✓ Review your personalized enrollment worksheet to see which healthcare options are available to you.
   - ✓ Read the At-a-Glance sheets to familiarize yourself with the main features of each plan.

2. Access the online Health Plan Decision Maker, and use the following:
   - ✓ Medical Plan Comparison Tool
   - ✓ Spending Accounts Tool

3. Enroll online or over the phone.
   - ✓ Go to [website] to enroll, or call the HR Service Center at XXX-XXX-XXXX.
   - ✓ Be sure to enroll by November 15.

4. Review your confirmation statement.
   - ✓ Make sure that your benefits elections and dependent information are correct.
   - ✓ If your information is incorrect, call the HR Service Center.

### Axe the Deadwood

Another way to reduce copy into meaningful chunks is to axe the deadwood. Whenever you see an empty word or phrase, replace it or delete it. Pretend every word costs you one dollar out of your paycheck, and suddenly, you'll find yourself editing like never before.

For example, cross out every "In the event of" you see and replace it with the wonderfully brief equivalent "If . . . ."

A good rule is that if you would not say a phrase aloud to another person, don't put it in writing.

### Open the LATCH to Organize Your Writing Better

Need help figuring out how to create a bulleted list, checklist, or table? We gain inspiration from Richard Saul Wurman, author of *Information Anxiety*,[1] who notes that there are five, and only five, ways to organize information. They are best remembered by the acronym LATCH, which stands for the following:

- **Location.**   This describes where certain things are in relation to others. For example, during orientation to a new job, it's useful for an employee to know where the cafeteria and restroom are, and where to find various departments or offices.
- **Alphabet.**   This isn't a great way to organize a grocery store, but it sure makes sense on the spice rack. Many topics benefit from being looked at from A to Z.
- **Time.**   The timeline is a great way to present historical information or to project into the future. It is an especially good device to summarize what benefits kick in when, or to show what happens to some benefits while an employee works for the company and when he retires.
- **Category.**   Most stores organize similar items together. This technique also works well when you're writing about certain HR programs, policies, or benefits. For example, a communication about time off might include programs that are administered by several different HR departments, but that distinction isn't of interest to an employee. She just wants to know the different situations in which she can take time off and how much time off she gets.
- **Hierarchy.**   Organizing from the bottom up or the top down—from smallest to largest, or most expensive to least—works well on its own or in combination with a category approach.

## *Use Plain Language*

Many of us who have worked in HR for a long time are suscepti-
ble to a syndrome known as "The Curse of Knowledge." Chip Heath
and Dan Heath describe this syndrome in their book *Made to Stick*:
"Once we know something, we find it hard to imagine what it was like
not to know it. Our knowledge has 'cursed' us."[2] The result is that we
write content that's too technical, so it's difficult for anyone who is not
an expert to understand.

Luckily, you can cure yourself of this curse in several ways. The
first is to stop using jargon that no one but you and your other subject
matter experts find interesting. Second, you can get rid of any and all
words and terms that are difficult to understand. For instance:

| Instead of: | Try: |
| --- | --- |
| Leverage | Use, employ, apply, exercise |
| Capability | Skill, talent, ability |
| Implement | Do, apply, put into practice |
| Integrate | Mix, combine, merge |
| Enable or facilitate | Allow, make possible, help, aid, assist |
| Input | Participate, contribute, take part, share |
| Innovative | New, original, fresh, novel, creative |

But you might protest that you must use specific HR terms
because they're the only way to accurately describe certain things, or
because they're legally required. If this is the case, you must not
assume that the average (or even above-average) employee understands these terms. Instead, define the term—and, even better, provide a quick glossary.

## Define Terms in a Sidebar for Easy Reference

In creating an open enrollment package, we included a glossary of terms that were somewhat familiar, yet might still cause employees some confusion. Here's a sample:

- **Copayment.** The flat dollar amount you pay when you visit a doctor or have a prescription filled.

- **Deductible.** The amount you pay each calendar year before you begin to receive reimbursements from the plan.

- **Out-of-pocket maximum.** Limits on the amount of money you or a covered dependent must pay toward eligible medical expenses in a calendar year. Once you reach that limit, the plans pay 100% of the allowed amount for the rest of the year.

- **Precertification.** A requirement that you or your health-care provider must notify your medical plan before you receive certain medical services.

*A Good Test for Simple Language*

How do you know if your language is simple enough? Check your readability. The average American reads at a 9th grade level, so some companies use that as a guide (as do publications such as *Reader's Digest*).

But an HR communicator we admire recently convinced senior management that all employee communication at her company needs to be written at a 7th grade level, which happens to be the level of most marketing (including ads created by her company). Her research showed that the 7th grade level is easiest for employees to understand. As she tells it, "We're not 'dumbing down' anything. We're making information accessible to everyone."

To check your readability using Microsoft Word, first open the Preferences menu and then the Spelling and Grammar section. Make

CHAPTER 5 • WRITE SIMPLY AND CLEARLY

sure that "Show readability statistics" is checked. Now, when you're drafting or editing a Word document, go to the Tools menu and choose "Spelling and Grammar." Run your document through the spelling and grammar checking process (always a good idea, anyway). At the end, a window will pop up that shows your Flesch-Kincaid grade level score. If it's 12th grade or above, your writing is probably too complex.

### *How to Keep It Short and Simple*

Here are some rules of thumb:

- Keep sentences at about 14 words.
- Limit paragraphs to three to four sentences.
- Create articles (in print or on the web) that run only 300 words or less.
- Use three to seven words in headlines.


## *Be Concrete*

Here's the first sentence of a bad job description that we suspect confused rather than attracted candidates:

> We're looking for a business/marketing expert who is a strategic and creative thinker with a natural ability to translate complex technical concepts into business results-oriented narratives that resonate with the organization, business, and industry.

This lead sentence is a lot of sound and fury, signifying nothing. It's an overload of jargon, and it doesn't begin to answer the basic question: What will the person in this job actually *do*? (By the way, this is just the beginning of the bad job description; you can see the whole horrible thing in Chapter 10, "Recruiting.")

When confronted with poor information like this (which you often are), your best tactic is to ask a lot of questions. The answers will give you information you need to change the vague to the concrete.

To create a meaningful job description for the job just mentioned, you'd want to know who this person would report to, how many people he or she would supervise, what the main deliverables are, when they are due, what groups the person would work with, how much time he or she would spend on different activities, and so on.

Collect concrete, specific examples and stories, describe how the person in the job will spend most of his or her time, and note special skills or expertise that will be valued. You'll have a job description that will attract qualified candidates.

### Tell Me a Story

One of the best ways to make communication concrete is to tell personal stories. Like photos, they are worth a thousand words. If I can find one person with a story that will make my life easier, make me more productive, make me happier at work, that's much more tangible than all the abstract terms you can muster.

We are all interested in personal stories because we realize, "Here's someone just like me" or "Here's someone I admire."

In some HR communications, you can feature real employees telling real stories—and that will make your communications much more powerful. But employees may not want to talk about certain topics. You can still tell the story; just don't use the person's real name or details.

## A Short Story

A benefits director wanted to "bring life insurance to life" to make it meaningful to employees. But she knew she couldn't use an actual employee's story. So she created a fictional character (based on a real situation) to illustrate the need for insurance and to show how reasonable the costs were:

Brenda is 45 years old and makes $40,000 a year. She is a single mom with two kids who worries about their financial well-being if something were to happen to her. To ease her mind, Brenda is choosing Voluntary Group Universal Life coverage for herself at 2.5 times her annual earnings, or $100,000. The coverage costs $0.126 per $1,000 for Brenda's age group, so her contribution is $12.60 per month.

# Checklist for Writing Simply

To make sure your message is perfectly clear, you'll want to master "sailing the seven Cs." When you've finished writing (or when you review someone else's writing), ask yourself if your writing is

- ✓ **Clear**—Is it easy to understand?
- ✓ **Concise**—Is it as brief as it can be?
- ✓ **Comprehensive**—Does it include all the necessary topics?
- ✓ **Complete**—Does it include all the necessary details?
- ✓ **Correct**—Is the information accurate?
- ✓ **Credible**—Does it add up?
- ✓ **Conversational**—Does it sound like a real person talking?

# 6

## Leverage Visuals

*In this chapter, you learn how to*

- *Apply visual techniques to enhance communication—even if you're not artistic*
- *Use text treatments to eliminate boring gray type*
- *Leverage charts and tables to organize information*
- *Tell an instant story using photography*
- *Put icons to work as an information shortcut*
- *Build an infographic to capture complex topics in a visual way*

As we explain in Chapter 5, "Write Simply and Clearly," there's no doubt that clear writing is a key component of effective communication. But another element is just as important, yet it's one that's often overlooked. This element is—you guessed it—visuals.

The more we understand about the workings of the human mind, the more we see the importance of visuals. For example, half the brain is devoted (directly or indirectly) to vision. We process images 60,000 times faster than text. Even letters and words are experienced visually: We learn the alphabet by associating A with apple, B with ball, and so on. When we read the letters "b-a-l-l," we don't process them individually. Rather, we "see" an image of the entire word—and we instantly associate the word with a mental picture of a bouncing sphere.

Marketers and the media leverage visuals to sell their products and convey ideas to an increasingly diverse world. Plus, because our world is overloaded with information, these persuaders know that visuals quickly cut through the clutter to capture people's attention and influence their thinking.

# Visuals Persuade

Presenters who use visuals are 43% more effective in persuading audience members to take a desired course of action than presenters who don't use visuals, according to a study by the University of Michigan School of Management.

Perhaps as a result, visuals are growing in importance in our society. From advertising to entertainment, from highway signs to retail store displays, visuals dominate. Writes Paul Martin Lester, Ph.D., professor at California State University at Fullerton, "Images . . . fill our newspapers, magazines, books, clothing, billboards, computer monitors, and television screens as never before in the history of mass communications." As a result, "We are becoming a visually mediated society. For many, understanding of the world is being accomplished, not through reading words, but by reading images."[1]

## *Leverage Visuals to Help Employees Understand*

What does this mean to you? Quite simply, visuals need to be one of your key communication strategies. And even if you can't draw, don't think of yourself as a visual person, and don't have the budget to hire a graphic designer, you can make communication more appealing through the simple use of visual techniques.

# Visuals Explain

Dan Roam, author of *The Back of the Napkin*, is a strong advocate of the impact of even the simplest visuals. As he puts it, "Visual thinking means taking advantage of our innate ability to see—both with our eyes and with our mind's eye—in order to discover ideas that are otherwise invisible, develop those ideas quickly and intuitively, and then share those ideas with other people in a way that they simply 'get.'"[2]

## Climb the Visual Tree

The first step in using visuals to enhance your communication is to understand the Visual Tree, a concept created by Alison's colleague David Pitre to illustrate the array of visual approaches available to us (see Figure 6-1).

We start at the bottom of the tree, before visuals, when all we have are words. But as we work our way up, we see the increasingly sophisticated visual options, leading all the way to the top, to moving images such as video and animation.

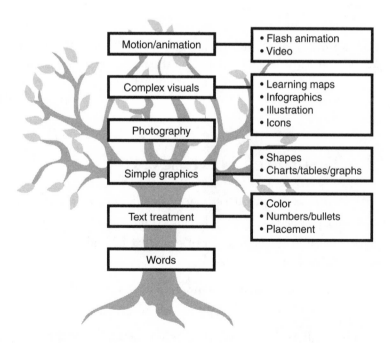

**Figure 6-1  The Visual Tree**

We show you how to use five branches of the Visual Tree—text treatment, simple graphics, photography, icons, and infographics—to make your communication more compelling. We give you tips on how to achieve many of these methods with available tools such as Microsoft Word and your digital camera. And we provide examples of applying visuals to a common HR communication challenge: providing information to employees during open enrollment.

### Learn More

New to using visuals? Here are two ways to learn more:

- **Observe.** As Yogi Berra once said, "You can observe a lot just by watching." Visit your favorite shopping website to see how designers use colors, images, and even white space to make merchandise appealing. Browse through a consumer magazine and notice the use of type treatments. Next time you're at the supermarket, pay attention to how the packaging is designed to draw you in.
- **Explore.** Much information about visuals is available for free on the Internet, including an About.com learning section on design basics, a website about color (www.colormatters.com), and even videos on YouTube that give the history of graphic design.

# Take Text to the Next Level

We love words as much as the next person; in fact, our ideal vacation includes a beach and a book. But even people like us don't want to have to search through a sea of gray text to find information we need when we need it.

So the first step in making your content more visual is by giving it a "text treatment"—breaking up the wall of words:

- Use bullets, numbers, and other chunking techniques, as demonstrated in Chapter 5.
- Give your text some oomph by using **boldface** or *italics*, making headlines or subheads larger.

- Break the boundaries of black and white by using color to high-light text.

In Figure 6-2, a communication about a change in a medical plan is made easier to read by using the framing techniques we show you in Chapter 4, "Frame Your Message," and the writing approaches described in Chapter 5. Then a text treatment—subheads in boldface type—is employed to enhance the look of the piece and make it easy to scan.

## New medical plans begin January 1, 2011

The company is making key changes to our medical plans designed to manage costs and simplify our offerings, starting with the Comprehensive Medical Plan.

### Comprehensive Medical Plan will become Comprehensive PPO
This change preserves valued plan features while offering cost-saving opportunities:

**Freedom to seek care from any health care provider**
The new plan will cover in-network care at the same rate of 70 percent. Participants may continue to seek out-of-network care, covered at 60 percent of the allowed amount.

**Better discounts in-network**
Because this plan will now be part of Aetna PPO network, participants in most locations will benefit from better provider discounts, which means lower out-of-pocket costs for in-network care.

**Same deductibles**
The savings we will realize by changing to the PPO network enables the company to maintain current deductibles and out-of-pocket maximums for 2011. Both in-network and out-of-network care will count toward deductibles and out-of-pocket maximums.

**Improved preventive care coverage**
All preventive care will continue to be covered at 70 percent of the allowed amount (60 percent out-of-network), even before the annual deductible is met.

**Figure 6-2   Using typography**

### *Beware the Typography Trap*

One common mistake that many nondesigners make is to overdo the use of typography fonts. (A font is a set or family of typefaces, such as Arial or Times New Roman.) After all, it's so easy to replace one font with another—and even to use a different font for every word in a sentence. But there are two very good reasons not to indulge in font madness. First, although occasional use of a different font creates interest, too many competing fonts are just distracting. And second, most organizations have guidelines that specify which fonts support your brand; you want your communication to be consistent with your company's look and feel.

To **emphasize many items, you** <u>underline</u> or use **boldface** for everything you think is **important**, but pretty soon your sentence looks **stressed out** and you've actually made it **harder to read**.

Another effective way to call attention to a point you want to make is to put some

white space

around it. For some reason, the eye just zooms in to that big empty space to see what gem is sitting there.

## Put Simple Graphics to Work

We're ready to climb the Visual Tree to the next branch, where you can find simple graphics such as shapes, charts, tables, and graphs.

We start with familiar shapes: squares, rectangles, ovals, and circles. "Shapes are at the root of graphic design," writes designer Eric Miller on About.com. "They are figures and forms that make up logos, illustrations, and countless other elements in all types of designs."

How should you consider using shapes? The simplest way is through the use of charts and tables to organize, connect, and separate information. In Figure 6-3, a complicated set of information—the differences between this year's PPO health plan and next year's plan—is neatly contained within a table. The shapes at work are just squares and rectangles, but they lead the reader's eye to find the facts he or she is looking for.

## Changes to PPO plan

| | Current PPO plans | | New PPO plan |
|---|---|---|---|
| | 2010 Basic | 2010 Select | 2011 Enhanced |
| Office visit copayment | • $20 non-specialist<br>• $40 specialist | • $20 non-specialist<br>• $40 specialist | • $25 non-specialist<br>• $40 specialist |
| Outpatient coverage | 85% coinsurance with an out-of-pocket maximum ($2,400 individual/ $4,800 family) | 100% coinsurance | 90% coinsurance with an out-of-pocket maximum ($1,250 individual/ $2,500 family) |
| Inpatient coverage | 85% coinsurance | $250/day copay with an 8-day copay maximum ($2,000) per year | $500/day copay with a 2-day copay maximum ($1,000) per year |

**Figure 6-3   Using tables**

Shapes also serve as symbols, providing visual shortcuts for key concepts:

❊ signifies something special

**X** marks the spot or indicates "don't"

✓ invites you to check something off your list

☆ tells you to pay attention, often because something's on sale

■ conveys balance

# Take a Picture

Visit any news website (CNN, *USA Today*, BBC), and what's the first thing you see? A photo that conveys today's top story. Stand in front of a newsstand, and what attracts your eye? Cover photos of celebrities, models, and, in the case of food magazines, a delicious meal. Look at today's newspaper, and what do you notice first? Even in the case of traditionally "gray" newspapers such as *The New York Times* and the *Wall Street Journal*, the most prominent feature on the front page is a large and evocative photo.

If, as Dr. Lester from the University of California says, we're living in a "visually mediated society," the medium most often used is photography. Ever since the advent of digital photography (and the ability of most mobile phones to snap a photo), nearly everyone's communicating with pictures instead of words. Visit a popular 20-year-old's Facebook page, and you'll see photos of him, his friends, his travels, and even what he ate for lunch.

How should you use photographs in your HR communication? We recommend two ways: stock photography and photos of employees.

## Stock Photography

Stock photos are, according to Webopedia, "professional photographs of common places, landmarks, nature, events, or people" that photographers provide to a service that then makes them available for sale. Sometimes stock services act as a paid library—you can "rent" the photo for one specific use—and sometimes the service is more like a bookstore, where you buy the photo and use it as you see fit.

The advantage of stock photography is that, for a reasonable price (and sometimes even for free) you can find nearly any photo you need, from a laughing baby to a piggy bank. And you can always locate photos of people who look like employees, to create communications employees can relate to.

In Figure 6-4, an article about a new life insurance option has been made more interesting by including a photo of a little girl holding an umbrella. The idea is to convey protection and to associate insurance with sheltering people you love.

## Protect your family with voluntary life insurance

Now you have a better way to protect your family with the company's enhanced volutary life insurance coverage.

As a result of this change you will be able to:

**1.** Increase your coverage amount to up to eight times annual salary

**2.** Reduce your contributions by approximately 20 percent

**3.** Increase your coverage level by up to one times annual pay each year during Open Enrollment without submitting evidence of good health

**Figure 6-4 Stock photography**

The downside of stock photos, of course, is that those smiling people aren't really employees. So you have to decide which is better: the convenience and professionalism of stock photos, or the authenticity of having pictures of your actual employees.

*Stock Photo Sources*

Search the web for "stock photo," and you'll find dozens of services available. Here are the three most often used by graphic designers we know:

- **iStockphoto** is a comprehensive stock photo service where members contribute content (which, in addition to photos, includes illustrations, video, and Flash animation). iStockphoto has many people photos in its collection, and the costs are reasonable: You can buy low-resolution images for a website or PowerPoint for as little as $1 per image.

- **Shutterstock** is a subscription-only collection, so you pay a monthly rate that allows you to download a certain number of photos. If you're a regular buyer of stock photos, and you need a large collection to choose from, Shutterstock may be for you.
- **Veer** is at the top of the price range, but it also offers the most sophisticated photos and illustrations.

## Employee Photos

We remember a time when the only way to obtain photos of your employees was to hire a professional photographer and arrange a photo shoot. Although that's certainly still an option—one of our clients just made the investment to illustrate a printed piece about culture change—digital photography gives you lots of other ways to include real-people photos in your communications.

Along the way, expectations about the quality of photos have changed. With the growth of social media—especially networking sites such as Facebook and content-sharing sites such as YouTube, SlideShare, and Flickr—we've all gotten more relaxed. The philosophy is that it's better for photos and videos to be "real" than to be perfect. You can be the photographer and take the photos you need—by getting out your digital camera and and asking employees to say "cheese"—or you can reach out to employees and ask them to submit their own photos. For example, you can ask parents to share baby photos to use in your maternity leave communication. Or suggest that active employees provide photos of themselves exercising to promote a wellness program. Use your creativity (and invite employees to do the same), and you'll find endless possibilities for picturing employees (by encouraging them to create the photos).

## Illustrate the Specific Point You Want to Make

If you have the budget to work with illustrators, they offer you another way to make your point clearly and quickly. What's great about illustrations is that you can show something it would be difficult to photograph (such as an accident happening), and you can include just the information that makes your point. Look at a variety of magazines and newspapers, and notice which stories benefit from illustrations and which from photographs, and then take your cues from the professionals.

# Create Shortcuts Using Icons

We're now ready to ascend to the upper branches of the Visual Tree to the mighty icon, which the Merriam Webster dictionary defines as "a pictorial representation: an image, emblem, or symbol." Or, as Alison wrote in her book, *Your Attention, Please*, an icon is "a small, easy-to-recognize image that is universally understood." Think about the image on a restroom door signifying men or women. Or the recycling symbol. Or how an outline of a folder indicates a location on your computer for storing files.

We like how designer and graphics instructor Jennifer Farley describes icons: "From the hieroglyphics on the pyramids of ancient Egypt to the orange RSS icon now gracing so many websites, icons have been used in both print and in web design . . . to draw the eye quickly to important parts of the document or web page."

The advantage of icons, says Ms. Farley, is that they "convey lots of information quickly" and can be used to grab people's attention or to rapidly communicate an idea.

We find lots of uses for icons in HR communication. For example, the enrollment communication shown in Figure 6-5 introduces an icon for each plan component: healthcare, dental, and vision. Throughout the rest of this enrollment package, which employees received at home, the icons reappear every time information is conveyed about that particular plan. And when employees visit the HR website, those icons appear again to provide a quick way for employees to find information about each plan. Icons therefore become a convenience for employees; they don't even have to read words to locate what they're looking for.

## Understanding your benefits

| Benefit Plan | Current Benefit | 2011 Benefit Change | What you need to do |
|---|---|---|---|
| Comprehensive Medical Plan | Deductibles: Individuals: $400 Family: $800 | Deductibles: Individuals: $800 Family: $1,600 | Consider contributing to the Health Care Spending Account to use before-tax money to pay your deductible for eligible expenses. |
| Dental Plan | Preventive care covered at 90%. | Preventive care covered at 100%. | Take advantage of preventive dental screenings to keep your teeth and gums healthy. |
| Vision Care Plan | Not available as a stand-alone plan. | New Vision Care Plan available on a before-tax contributory basis, including benefits for eye examinations and eyewear. | Consider enrolling in the Vision Care Plan. Visit [website URL] for more information. |

Figure 6-5    Using icons

# Make Complex Concepts Simple Through Infographics

Imagine that you were just appointed commissioner of a new transit system in your city that combines buses and light rail trains that connect to the Amtrak train station and the airport. You need to communicate to riders how they can get from point A to point B, which often involves transferring from one vehicle to another.

What's the best way to do so? Ideally, the solution would be a single page that riders could carry with them as they travel. This page also would become a poster displayed at bus stops and ticket windows, and an image posted on your system's website.

What you need, of course, is something like the New York City subway map, which uses a visual system for showing routes, modes of transportation, and where all those vehicles go.

That visual system is known as an information graphic, or infographic. And the best definition we found was on Wikipedia (yes, we know, not always the most reliable source): "Infographics are visual representations of information, data, or knowledge. These graphics are used where complex information needs to be explained quickly and clearly."

Wikipedia goes on to give examples of infographics:

* In newspapers, such as *USA Today*, they're used to show the weather as well as maps and site plans for newsworthy events.
* In scientific literature, they illustrate physical systems, such as cutaway views of anatomy, astronomical diagrams, and images of microscopic systems.
* Transit systems use infographics to integrate a variety of information such transfer points and local landmarks.

The more complex your information, the more you should consider creating an infographic. For example, if your performance management system has a lot of moving parts—goal setting, mid-year review, year-end review, calibration, bonus calculation—an infographic could be created to capture all the components. Then it could be shared with your HR team or managers so that they clearly understand how the system works.

In Figure 6-6, an infographic helps convey the details of maternity leave. The organizing principle is time. In this company, a typical maternity leave spans 14 weeks—two weeks before the baby is born and 12 weeks afterward. So the infographic is organized to show pay and leave choices the employee might make during the period.

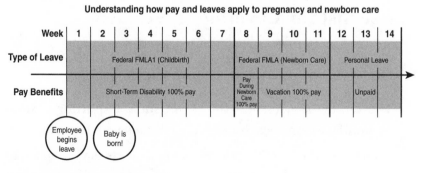

**Figure 6-6   Infographic**

# When You Don't Have Money for Graphic Designers

If you don't have the budget to work with a graphic designer, and yet you know you really could use a professional's help, here are two suggestions:

First, get recommendations of talented graphic designers from communication professionals in other companies. Then meet with a few designers to see if they would agree to a single-time fee to create a template you could use for all your communication needs. Or perhaps you could offer something that would be an incentive for the designer to give you a price break (sometimes it can be as simple as a credit line). If you can get a price break, approach your management with evidence to persuade them that working with a specific designer would be a good investment.

The second suggestion (which we mention briefly in Chapter 3, "Plan and Manage Communication") is to visit a local college that teaches graphic design. Ask one or more instructors if your need for communication design or illustration could become a class project. This would be a win-win situation. The students would see what it's like to work in the real world, the student whose work is selected would have a work sample before graduation, and you would get a great design or illustration for free.

# Checklist for Leveraging Visuals

Now that you've climbed the Visual Tree, you're ready to leverage visuals in your communication. Keep in mind the following:

✓ Even the simplest text treatment (**such as putting text in boldface**) can make your communication more interesting.

✓ You can use simple graphics—tables, charts, and shapes—to organize information, make it easier to access, and give it more energy.

✓ A compelling visual is as close as your digital camera or the photo-taking abilities of your employees.

✓ When time is of the essence, icons are an effective shortcut.

✓ Whether you're navigating the subways or helping people understand complicated HR systems, infographics make the complex simple.

# 7

## Use the Right Tool for the Job

*In this chapter, you learn*

- *Pros and cons of different communication tools*
- *Why a mix of media works best in many situations*
- *How to make the best use of each communication vehicle*

You're frustrated. You've just returned to your desk after spending 90 minutes at a meeting where you learned a single fact that easily could have been communicated in an e-mail. Now, as you try to catch up on your e-mail, you open a long message that leaves you with more questions than answers. You go online to watch a video that lasts eight painful minutes and doesn't tell you anything you didn't already know. A colleague asks for feedback on a poster, designed to be displayed outside the cafeteria. It contains so much information that it can only be read by someone standing six inches away.

We call this syndrome "Bad Use of Communication Tools." Too often communication falls short because people use the wrong tool for the job. Perhaps they send an e-mail when a conversation is needed, or call a meeting just to provide background information. This is the equivalent of picking up a hammer when you need to drill a hole.

### A Thought About Tools

*"I think the hard thing about tools is that it takes a fair amount of effort to become proficient."*

—Bill Joy, computer scientist and cofounder of Sun Microsystems

A second mistake is to choose the right communication tool but misuse it. Examples of this problem include an e-mail as lengthy as an employee handbook or a meeting that's all presentation and no discussion. This is like using a hammer to drive a nail, but hitting the nail so hard that it cracks the plaster.

This chapter helps you do it right by showing you how to choose the appropriate communication tool. It also gives you tips on making that tool work for you and your employee audience.

# Review the Tools in Your Tool Kit

Let's start by understanding the pros and cons of each tool:

| Tool | What It's Right For | What It's Wrong For |
|---|---|---|
| E-mail | Quick, actionable information | Providing detailed information, communicating tough topics |
| Website | Comprehensive information available anytime, opportunities for employees to connect with one another | Urgent information |
| Print (brochure, newsletter) | Telling a story, putting issues into context | News |
| Workplace communication (posters, bulletin boards) | Quick reminder or overview | Details, context |
| Audio (podcasts or CDs) | Bringing an issue to life, telling a story | Complex information, anything best conveyed visually |
| Video | Dramatizing and illustrating an issue | In-depth information |
| Meetings (face-to-face or virtual) | Explaining complex content, answering questions | One-way delivery |
| Social media, such as Facebook, wikis, blogs | Connecting employees to each other | Broadcasting "official" information |

By knowing what each tool does best, you can begin deciding how to use each one for the communication you have planned.

But before you jump in, we remind you of two important steps:

1. **Consider employees' communication needs and preferences** (see Chapters 1, "Know Your Employees," and 2, "Treat Your Employees Like Customers"). For example, if your sales force consists mostly of Millennials, those employees will probably prefer electronic communication over print (or even face-to-face). And they'll expect to find information easily and get their questions answered quickly.

2. **Revisit your objectives** (see Chapter 3, "Plan and Manage Communication") to make sure you focus on what you need employees to know, believe, and do. By doing so, you'll make sure your choice of vehicles will accomplish your objectives.

# Deciding on the Best Tool

Here are examples of how an HR manager might match employee needs, objectives, and the appropriate communication vehicle:

| Employee Need | Your Objective | The Right Tool | Example |
|---|---|---|---|
| "I want to talk about healthcare options at home with my family." | Employees make the best decision about healthcare and enroll on time | Print | Open enrollment mailing |
| "I need to figure out what I'll receive from my 401(k) retirement account when I retire." | Employees fully participate in the 401(k) plan | Website | Retirement benefit estimator |

*continued*

| Employee Need | Your Objective | The Right Tool | Example |
|---|---|---|---|
| "I want to understand how our bonus program is changing and what it means to me." | Employees understand the change and don't overwhelm HR with inquiries | Meeting | Face-to-face or virtual sessions to explain changes and answer employee questions |
| "Show me how all our different policies and benefits work together when my baby arrives." | Affected employees know what the benefits and policies are and take appropriate action | A one-pager (in print or online) | A chart or graphic that shows all relevant information about maternity leave |
| "I have a lot of questions about disability insurance." | Employees enroll in long-term disability | A live chat | An instant-messaging session in which employees ask questions and get an immediate response from an expert |

## Celebrating Your New and Improved Dental Plan

Is a toothbrush a communication tool? Not usually, but you can use a toothbrush—or a T-shirt or pedometer or other object—to call attention to what you need to communicate. For example, when one client announced an improved dental plan, we recommended giving away toothbrushes in travel cases. The result? The requests for more toothbrushes exceeded the number of employees. (In short, people loved them.)

The secret to using nontraditional tools? Make sure that the object is something relevant—a key chain doesn't communicate wellness—and that it's something employees will value. You don't need to conduct a survey to find this out; a small number of informal conversations with typical employees will give you the feedback you need.

# Using Each Tool Effectively

Now that you know how to choose your tools, we show you how to enhance the way you use some of the most common vehicles: e-mail, print publications, and posters and bulletin boards. We also include tips on the newest form of communication: social media. (We cover face-to-face communication in Chapter 8, "Make Meetings Meaning-ful—and Support Managers.")

## *E-mail: Love It, Hate It, Need It*

Ah, e-mail. We love e-mail's ease of use, speed, and responsive-ness. But we hate the feeling of being besieged by a never-ending onslaught of incoming messages.

## *How Many E-mails?*

According to The Radicati Group, a technology marketing research firm, here's why you feel overloaded:

- 90 trillion: The number of e-mails sent in 2009
- 247 billion: The average number of e-mails sent each day
- 1.4 billion: The number of e-mail users worldwide
- 81%: The percentage of e-mails that were spam

Because employees receive so much e-mail, they've become skilled at deciding in seconds whether to press the Delete key or open a message and keep reading. How can you make sure your e-mails don't get thrown in the trash? Here are a few tips:

- Use e-mail only when information is timely and action is required.
- Clearly outline action steps.
- Write strong, direct subject lines that summarize what you're conveying.

- Use the inverted pyramid (see Chapter 4, "Frame Your Message") to organize the body of your message.

- Rely on bullet points, numbers, and other devices (see Chapter 5, "Write Simply and Clearly") to chunk your message into easily digestible bits.

- Limit your message to a single screen.

## To the Point

When the economy took a nosedive in 2008, the Compensation and Benefits department at a major corporation began hearing from employees that they were anxious about their rapidly diminishing retirement funds. So the department asked the company's accounting firm to offer seminars on financial planning.

Since the subject was so compelling, we knew we could keep the message simple and still get employees' attention. Here is the e-mail we wrote:

*Subject line:*

Have questions about your finances? Get answers at this workshop.

*Message body:*

Acme is partnering with our accounting firm, Smith & Smith, to offer free workshops on Financial Planning in Uncertain Times. Led by certified financial planners, the group sessions will offer insights into how you can adjust your financial strategies to respond to a weak economy.

Workshops will be held between May 1 and July 2 at many locations and via the web on Live Meeting.

For a full schedule, visit [link]. To sign up, visit the website or call XXX-XXX-XXXX.

### Graphic E-mails Get Attention

What's better than even the best text e-mail? If you have time and resources, consider creating a "graphic e-mail." This designed e-mail (programmed using HTML, the same code used to create websites) looks like an ad when the recipient opens it. You're probably familiar with graphic e-mails, because you receive them from online retailers such as Lands' End, Victoria's Secret, and The Gap to advertise special offers such as free shipping.

Graphic e-mails (which some people call "e-cards" because they're like electronic postcards) allow you to communicate a simple idea (see Figure 7-1). That way, employees don't have to read a text message; they can quickly scan the "ad." E-cards can be used to communicate the following:

- Dates and deadlines, such as the beginning and end of open enrollment, or the deadline for submitting a Flexible Spending Account claim
- Events, such as upcoming sessions about healthcare plans or retirement programs
- One compelling message, to reinforce or link to more comprehensive information on an intranet site

**Figure 7-1 A graphic e-mail**

### Another Thought About Tools

*"Man is a tool-using animal. Without tools he is nothing; with tools he is all."*

—Thomas Carlyle, 19th century Scottish writer

## *(Still) Powerful Print*

About a decade ago, print was nearly extinct as an internal communication channel. Companies had invested so much in their intranets that they cut budgets for other forms of communication. The environmental movement was on the rise, and it seemed wrong to "kill all those trees." (See the sidebar "The Truth About Killing Trees" in Chapter 3.) And, let's face it, print took a lot of work to do well.

As a result, many organizations eliminated print. But then something strange happened. HR people began to notice that employees were calling more often, because they didn't understand key programs as well. After one company stopped producing and mailing open enrollment packages, the HR director discovered that employees were covertly printing dozens of pages from the intranet site (which, by the way, cost the company a lot more money than if the material had been sent to a printer). Other clients realized that eliminating print was unfair to employees who had limited electronic access.

Consider print's value to certain employee segments:

| Segment | Why Print Works |
|---|---|
| Manufacturing or retail | Many workers have limited access to e-mail and the intranet and may be uncomfortable with technology. |
| Call center | They have computers but have little time during working hours to read e-mail or browse the intranet. |
| Remote workers | People such as sales representatives, flight attendants, and service technicians prefer portable communication that they can stick in their bag and peruse when they have a few minutes. |
| Technology | It may seem counterintuitive, but IT and other technology workers find that print gives them a break from screen time. |

As a result, print has returned to its rightful place in the toolbox, especially for communicating complex information such as enrollment options. And that's good news, because print has been proven to be more effective than electronic communication as a way to get people interested. (More good news: The cost of print has declined, and there are many "green" ways to print.)

Want an example of the power of print? A 2006 study of consumer behavior demonstrates that people are more engaged by print media such as newspapers and magazines than they are by electronic media such as TV, radio, and the Internet.

By "engagement," the authors—academic researchers at Ball State University's Center for Media Design—mean the amount of concentrated time that consumers spend on media. Known as the Middletown Media Studies,[1] the research is based on more than 5,000 hours of direct observation of consumers using media.

The upshot is that people are much more likely to devote their full attention to print publications than they are to other media. So although consumers spend far more time on TV, radio, and the Internet, they're likely to be multitasking. They might have two or more of these channels on at once, or might be using an electronic medium as "background noise" while involved in other activities. Can a study about external media be applied to internal communication? Absolutely, because employees use media in similar ways, no matter where the information comes from.

*Three Ways to Tap the Power of Print*

- **Make print service-oriented.** Print is an ideal medium for service journalism (described in Chapter 5). It can help employees understand key issues so that they can see where they fit and know how to make a contribution. Think "how to" and "news you can use."
- **Paint a picture.** Follow best practices from magazines to make your information visual using photographs, charts,

graphs, and other graphic elements. The most arresting visual of all? People's faces.

- **Give employees the choice of skimming or reading.** Depending on their interest in the topic, some of your readers will just scan—looking quickly at the headline, subheads, photo captions, and sidebars—and others will devour every word. Make sure your content is chunked to appeal to both.

---

**Still Another Thought About Tools**

*"Man must shape his tools lest they shape him."*

—Arthur Miller, playwright

---

## Waiting in the Cafeteria Line

Our next trip to the toolkit is for an often-neglected tool: workplace communication such as posters, bulletin board postings, and electronic signs and screens. Why would we care about these? Because even if your company has some virtual workers, most employees spend the majority of their time in the company's office, manufacturing plant, store, warehouse, or other facility. That means they walk through an entrance, clock in (if they're hourly workers), visit the restroom, and wait in line in the cafeteria. And while they do so, they could be getting valuable information by looking at posters, bulletin boards, or electronic signs or screens.

The best part about workplace communication is that, even if your budget is miniscule, you can create posters or bulletin boards. All you need is paper, some tacks or tape, and the know-how to get your message across.

## What's the Fastest-Growing Advertising Venue?

If you guessed television, radio, or even online, you'd be wrong. The two fastest-growing advertising venues are outdoor (billboards) and in-store (such as signs stuck on the floor and video screens near the cash register). Why? Because advertisers know they can catch their audience's attention when they are driving down the road or pushing a cart. A few facts:

- The world market for outdoor advertising was projected to reach $30.4 billion in 2010, a growth of 10%, according to Global Industry Analysts.

- Transit advertising is the fastest-growing outdoor advertising mode.

- "Digital signage" is the hottest trend in store displays. An array of retailers—from supermarkets to bookstores—are experimenting with these screens.

### High-Potential Posters

Poor posters. They have such potential, but they're often created quickly, without much thought. The result is often mediocre: they lack a strong visual element, are full of words, try to convey too much content, and are not compelling. And employees, who always know good communication when they see it, respond appropriately. Here are some employee comments from a focus group study we conducted recently at a manufacturing facility:

- "I never look at posters. They just don't seem relevant to me."
- "Posters here are terrible. You have to stand there and read them. Who has time for that?"
- "I glance at the posters on the way to the cafeteria, but most of them seem like they're just up so that someone can check something off their list—you know, 'I put it on a poster, so I communicated it.' But if no one pays attention, what's the point?"

This is a missed opportunity, because posters are such a great way to convey concepts to people where they pause and/or congregate: In the break room. Waiting outside the credit union. Standing in the elevator.

Posters are especially valuable for employees who don't have easy electronic access. But, as Hollywood film studios (think movie posters), advertisers (billboards), and retailers (visual displays) know, posters work for anyone. After all, we have to look at something, so it might as well be attractive, interesting, and persuasive.

For inspiration, look not within your own company, but at world-class posters. There's a great website about posters throughout history at www.artlex.com/ArtLex/p/poster.html. For a "greatest hits" list of movie posters over the last several years, go to www.impawards.com.

**Poster Tips**

- Always use a strong visual.
- Severely limit the number of words. (Headlines should be fewer than seven words.)
- Test whether a poster works by putting it on a wall, approaching it from the side, and walking by it at a normal pace.
- Hang posters at eye level in a variety of high-traffic areas.
- Keep posters up long enough so that employees notice them, but not so long that they become wallpaper.

*The Best Bulletin Boards*

We love bulletin boards because all you need to be successful is some cork board, a box of pushpins, and the ability to channel your inner third-grade teacher.

Here are a few rules of thumb for making the most of bulletin boards:

- **Create interest and engagement through colorful visuals.** Employees need information that is quick and easy to digest and understand. Visuals such as progress charts, diagrams, photographs, and posters support the need to "get it fast."

- **Target high-traffic locations.** While the size of your bulletin boards may vary depending on available space, what's critical is where they're located. Avoid positioning bulletin boards in narrow hallways, where the tendency is to walk past them without noticing. Instead, display bulletin boards in open areas where employees are more likely to stop and visit, such as the cafeteria or break room or near an elevator.

## Location, Location, Location

A major retailer had a comprehensive and effective employee communication program. But the HR director felt that communication in each store could use some improvement. So we went to visit several locations to explore what was going on. One of the first things we noticed was the bulletin boards. There were lots of them—some with specific themes (such as sales and promotions), and others of a more general nature. And the people who ran the bulletin boards took the assignment seriously: Most boards were colorful and creative.

There was just one problem: Almost every bulletin board was in the wrong place. One was located in a narrow, heavily trafficked hallway; it was unlikely that anyone would stop to look at the board and risk getting trampled. Another was at the very end of the locker room area, where no one ever went. And, worst of all, there was no bulletin board near the place every employee visited twice a day: the time clock.

Our advice? "We love your bulletin boards," we told the HR director. "But they're being wasted. If you move them, they'll be a lot more effective."

- **Develop a consistent architecture.** You need a blueprint to organize the information on your bulletin boards. Key content areas could include the following:
  - ✓ A calendar of upcoming meetings and events (local or corporate-wide)
  - ✓ Job safety policies
  - ✓ Employee recognition
  - ✓ Career development opportunities
  - ✓ Goals/strategies/performance results

- **Designate individuals to maintain the bulletin board(s) in their area/location.** This includes revising and/or replacing outdated information and collecting employee feedback if you have interactive features such as suggestion boxes.

# Everybody into the Pool!

An employee communication tool that's getting a lot of attention these days is social media. In case you're not completely familiar with this new-ish communication channel, we bring you a definition from Brian Solis, one of the gurus of social media marketing:

> **Social media** describes the online tools that people use to share content, profiles, opinions, insights, experiences, perspectives, and media itself, thus facilitating conversations and interaction online between groups of people. These tools include blogs, message boards, podcasts, microblogs, lifestreams, bookmarks, networks, communities, wikis, and vlogs.
>
> A few prominent examples of social media applications are Wikipedia (reference); MySpace and Facebook (social networking); Twitter and Jaikue (presence apps); YouTube (video sharing); Second Life (virtual reality); Upcoming (Events); Digg and Reddit (news aggregation); Flickr and Zooomr (photo sharing); Blogtv, Justin.tv, and Ustream (live-casting); Stickham and YourTrumanShow (episodic online

video); Izimi and Pownce (media sharing); del.icio.us (book-marking); and World of Warcraft (online gaming).[2]

If you're older than, say, 30, you may consider social media to be an activity mostly for the young. But social media is not just for kids. Although 18-to-29-year-olds are the largest users of social media, 43% of 30-somethings and 29% of 40-somethings use these tools—and the numbers keep increasing. For example, we've found that the business social network LinkedIn is more popular among people over 30, whereas there are more Facebook fans among Millennials (born between 1980 and 2000).

Despite the growing popularity of social media, many of us are unsure how to use this tool. After all, there are so many possibilities and quite a few risks. Here are a few suggestions for including social media in your communication program:

- **Be clear about your objectives.**   We know—we keep referring to objectives. That's because understanding what you're trying to accomplish is such a great way to focus—and to make good decisions about the best ways to communicate. Resist the temptation to launch social media because the cool kids are doing so. First, figure out how social media helps you get to where you need to go.

- **Don't go it alone.**   Social media isn't "owned" by anyone; it's bigger than any one function. So the best way to tackle social media is often to form a team that includes HR, IT, Legal, and Corporate Communications. By doing so, you can address all the aspects: technology, external reputation (all those crazy bloggers), policies, and employee engagement.

- **When you're ready to start, don't jump into the deep end; just dip your toe into the water.**   The nice thing about social media is that you can quietly experiment, see how it goes, and then ramp up or switch gears. Many tools are free or cheap, and commonly used IT platforms such as Microsoft SharePoint have social media options such as blogs and wikis built in.

- **Give it a go with recruiting.** As we explain in Chapter 10, "Recruiting," many companies start by supplementing their traditional recruiting communication efforts with Facebook, LinkedIn, and Twitter. It's a great way to get your feet wet while attracting potential employees who aren't reading newspaper classified ads.

- **Ask your employees what they use and what they need.** In the very early days of social media, we had several clients who enthusiastically plunged into creating internal Facebook-like networks. But some of these efforts failed; employees just didn't use them. What was the problem? As one employee told us, "I'm already on the real Facebook, where I connect with all my friends and colleagues. Why would I create a new profile and new connections when I don't need to?" Make sure you understand employees' preferences for how they would use internal social media channels.

- **Help employees solve problems and get work done.** Networking is fun, but your best employees are focused on doing their jobs. That's why many organizations are exploring social media's potential for making work easier. For example, a major pharmaceutical client has introduced Yammer, an internal microblog that works like Twitter. Employees form groups and then post comments or questions such as "Looking for data on how XX software can increase run time. Can anyone help?" or "Just ran a successful test using XX new methodology. Would be happy to share my results." When employees are located in multiple locations and a variety of time zones, they appreciate that Yammer is a great way to collaborate with colleagues and get work done despite geographic or time differences. Isn't that what it's all about?

---

### A Final Thought About Tools

*"A bad workman always blames his tools."*

—Proverb

---

# Summing Up: Put Every Tool to Work

When you're communicating something especially important, you'll want to include a variety of tools to help employees understand their options and make good choices.

When we helped a major pharmaceutical company communicate open enrollment in a year that included many changes, we recommended a communication program that included nearly every tool available: newsletters, fact sheet, postcards, posters, benefits fair, website enrollment, cafeteria tent cards, and plasma screen panels in major lobby locations. Here is how each tool contributed to the overall success of the open enrollment:

- **Newsletters** helped share complex subjects in short, easy-to-read segments, including charts, bullets, and lists.
- **The fact sheet** gave employees information in one concise page to encourage them to act. For example, one piece listed excuses employees might use to postpone enrolling ("I don't need it," "I can't afford it") and gave compelling reasons to act now.
- **Postcards** reminded employees that it was time to act. We used postcards for two different events. The first reminded employees to enroll, sharing website and phone information. The second focused on one aspect of enrollment: long-term disability.
- **Posters** were put up throughout facilities—outside cafeterias and lunchrooms, near elevators, at entrances, and on bulletin boards—to reinforce key messages.
- **A benefits fair** gave employees the chance to ask questions and get answers immediately.
- **Website or phone enrollment** offered employees a fast, simple, inexpensive way to enroll and to see immediately what their costs would be. Employees without web access could call a toll-free number to enroll.

- **Cafeteria tent cards** encouraged employees to "Enroll today."
- **Plasma screen panels** provided information about where employees could attend a benefits fair and reminded them of the upcoming deadline for enrollment.

# Checklist for Choosing the Right Tool for the Job

✓ Consider your audience and your message.

✓ Think about all the tools at your disposal (along with the pros and cons of each), and then determine how each might help you communicate a specific message.

✓ Make sure you're making the most out of each tool.

# 8

## Make Meetings Meaningful— and Support Managers

*In this chapter, you learn how to*

- *Improve meetings to realize their potential as an effective communication channel*
- *Make web/virtual meetings more dynamic and compelling*
- *Provide managers with information, tools, and skills to improve communication with their teams*

We've been around for a long time, so we remember the "good old days" before electronic communication made it possible to reach anyone anywhere at any time. And, although we mostly prefer today's communication, one aspect used to be better: meetings.

Since meetings are a key form of communication in most organizations, you'd expect them to be effective. But too often meetings are long, boring, and unproductive.

While it's not our intention to fix every meeting, we'd like to help you improve the meetings you hold to inform employees about HR programs, policies, and benefits. For example, many HR professionals we know invite employees to meetings during open enrollment to help them understand health plan changes. A defense company used meetings when it made radical changes to its retirement plan: The HR team traveled to all company locations and held a series of "road shows" to explain the new plan to employees. And it's a best practice to include web briefings or face-to-face sessions whenever the topic being communicated is complex or emotional.

After all, meetings can be the best channel for explaining complicated topics, providing context and allowing employees to get their questions answered.

In this chapter, we show you how to improve your meetings with employees (and, in fact, with anyone). We also provide advice on how you can help the most important communicators in your company— managers—improve their person-to-person communication.

# First, the Bad News

Alison goes to a lot of meetings. In fact, during a recent month she attended a gathering of a company's top 100 leaders, a session for a corporation's HR network, and a regional conference put on by a leading communication organization.

Her conclusion? Despite the fact that much great information was shared at these meetings, the planners had a lot to learn about creating dynamic and effective meetings. Here are just a few of the mistakes made:

- **Uncomfortable venue.** At one session, more than 100 attendees were shoehorned into a small, windowless room designed to hold no more than 70 people. As a result, participants were oxygen-deprived, cramped, and cranky.

- **Too many presentations.** PowerPoint presentations can be effective, but not when a daylong meeting consists of nothing but presentation after presentation. That's just mind-numbing.

- **Not enough visuals.** With all that PowerPoint, you'd think there'd be plenty to look at. Yet many meetings offer few visuals to break up the sea of words on slides.

- **Poor time management.** Speakers allowing no time for questions. Sessions running long, stealing time from later sessions, cutting into breaks, truncating lunch. Not enough time allocated to hold a breakout session. All are examples of poor time management, which ruins the meeting flow and causes participants to zone out.

- **Not enough dialogue.** If a meeting's only objective is to disseminate information, do yourself a favor, and save a bunch of time by publishing a report. But if the intention of your meeting is to create learning so that people can solve problems or take action, you must build opportunities for dialog into the agenda. That requires time, space, and planning.

# Our Mission for Meetings

Despite the fact that meetings often disappoint, we continue to have high hopes. In fact, meetings have such potential that we've created this mission statement for what we'd like them to be: **Meetings should not only share information but also engage, motivate, educate, and solve problems so that participants think and act differently as a result.**

Is this possible? Absolutely. We'll show you how.

### *Good Meetings Begin at the End*

By "the end," we mean outcomes: objectives you want to achieve by getting people together. The worst meetings contain a kitchen sink full of miscellaneous stuff, messy and without direction. By contrast, the best are focused, with a clear purpose. What's the difference? Having clear objectives, of course. (You know by now that we're big fans of objectives, and we recommend that you use them for meetings as well as other communication.)

To decide on your focus, set one to three objectives that address at least one of the following questions:

- What will participants learn by the end of this meeting? What decision will be made?
- How will participants think differently? What will they believe?
- What actions will participants take after the meeting? What will they do?

## Your Friend, the Agenda

After you've set your objectives, the best meetings are carefully designed to achieve them. The old-fashioned word for this design is "agenda," but you need to do more than create a bulleted list of content to cover. You should structure your meeting to have a flow that makes sense, build in opportunities for participants to—well, participate, and to manage time so that you get everything done.

To get started, think of your meeting as a television talk show. Channel your inner Oprah or Larry King. You'll need a dynamic host, interesting guests, supporting visuals, and opportunities for audience (participant) feedback. Your agenda becomes a guide that helps you do the following:

- Devote time to the things that matter most
- Set aside blocks of time for important topics
- Allow adequate time for recharging, informal discussion, and relationship building

### Come Together

During an economic downturn, a manufacturing plant went through some rough times: a product line was suspended, and employees were furloughed or their hours were cut. When business improved, the plant manager wanted to create an event that would bring employees together to focus on where the organization was headed and create understanding about what employees could do to contribute to the plant's success. The plant manager turned to the HR director for help. She created an agenda that included both presentations and opportunities for participation:

| Time | Content | Facilitator |
|------|---------|-------------|
| 9:00 a.m. | Introduction | Plant manager |
| 9:05 a.m. | Communicate the detailed vision and mission—where we're headed—and behaviors we need to focus on to get there<br><br>Answer questions | Plant manager |
| 9:45 a.m. | Identify strengths<br><br>Each table brainstorms three to five strengths (one per card) that will help us achieve the vision and mission<br><br>Table participants vote on one card and present it to the group<br><br>All cards are gathered, sorted, and prioritized into a Top 10 list | HR |
| 10:15 a.m. | Break | |
| 10:30 a.m. | Define attributes for the new way of working<br><br>Using flip chart paper, each table creates a mind map (a diagram of related words) of attributes we need to work differently<br><br>All participants draw on their table's page<br><br>Pages are displayed around the room<br><br>All pages are gathered and consolidated | HR |
| 11:30 a.m. | Identify obstacles and solutions<br><br>Using a flip chart, each table develops three to five obstacles or weaknesses<br><br>Teams develop a solution for each obstacle/opportunity (solutions can be practical or "blue sky")<br><br>Tables report on one obstacle/solution<br><br>Pages are gathered | HR |
| 12:15 p.m. | Lunch | |

*continued*

| Time | Content | Facilitator |
|------|---------|-------------|
| 12:45 p.m. | New-day resolutions | HR |
| | Using the day's learning, each participant writes down on two cards one thing he or she will do differently going forward ("I resolve to...") | |
| | All participants share their resolutions with a colleague | |
| | The management team share the resolutions with the whole room | |
| | All participants keep one card and turn in the other | |
| 1:00 p.m. | How we'll communicate with you going forward | Plant manager |
| | Aggregate all cards/docs from all sessions and draft a plan | |
| | Communicate update/results to employees in shift meetings next week | |
| | Follow up with town hall meetings in 30 days | |
| | Take questions | |
| 1:45 p.m. | Meeting close | |

## Set Participants' Expectations

As soon as you start your meeting, it's important to manage everyone's expectations, particularly if you plan to go beyond the typical static session.

To set expectations, at the beginning of the meeting let participants know the following:

- What you'll accomplish in this session (objective/outcomes)
- What you'll cover, including order and timing (agenda)
- What everyone in the meeting will do (roles)
- How you'll conduct the meeting (rules of the road)

## *Manage Information Sharing*

We're well aware that a key reason people hold meetings is to share information. But that doesn't mean you should take this process for granted. Effective information sharing is not just a matter of slapping together a PowerPoint deck. In fact, pinning your whole approach on PowerPoint can be a big mistake.

For example, recently a client visited us, asking for advice on the CEO town hall meetings she had just been put in charge of. The client opened a folder and pulled out a printout of a PowerPoint deck. "This is what the CEO has been doing," she said, straining as she lifted the thick stack and plunked it on the desk.

It was a car-wreck moment: We didn't want to look, but we had to. And the reality was worse than we feared: There were 55—count 'em—slides. And they weren't visual; these slides were chock-full of charts, graphs, and data.

"How long are your town hall meetings?" we asked the client.

"An hour," she replied.

"Any time for questions and answers?"

"Just a few minutes," she said. "But nobody asks any questions, anyway."

That wasn't surprising. After 50 minutes of this dizzying array of information, employees were brain-dead. The problem wasn't just the quantity of slides; it was how the meeting was organized. Nine separate topics were covered. Large quantities of data were reported. There were no stories, just thousands of facts.

Worst of all, none of it was directly relevant to the employees. There was no way for them to get involved, no call to action, no opportunity to do anything but passively sit in the audience, waiting for it to be over.

How should our client stop this information-sharing madness? Here's some advice:

- Start, of course, with objectives.
- Always keep participants' needs in mind. Ask yourself: What information is important to them? What do they need to know? Why? What do you want them to do with the information?
- Consider other methods of sharing information. PowerPoint's a default, but are there other options? Create a fact sheet or other handout? Do an interview-style Q&A? Design posters?
- Use *more* PowerPoint slides—but with a lot less content per slide. Keep each slide clean and simple. Avoid using too many slides with detailed information, dense with text and graphics. Instead, use slides to illustrate only the main points.

### *Create a Facilitation Approach*

If you're serious about making meetings meaningful, you need to go beyond passive presentations and create a truly interactive experience for participants. Doing so is worth the effort, because when participants have a chance to "work with" content, their retention increases.

Alison was reminded of the importance of interaction a couple of years ago when her youngest son, then a high school senior, was in the process of visiting prospective colleges.

Despite the fact that colleges are quite effective at communicating at a distance—via websites, print materials, and social media—their on-campus meetings can be terrible. Out of four colleges Alison and her son visited during one trip, two started their tours with a mind-numbing, worst-practice PowerPoint presentation, narrated by an Admissions geek.

The presentations were as bad as you'd find at any corporation: a series of slides with bulleted lists, with the presenter reading every word.

After the first three minutes, Alison's son whispered, "This is just for the parents, not for the kids."

Well, no, because she was as cranky as he was. So, to amuse herself, Alison began to silently consult on how to run the session better. There were about 15 prospective students (and about 20 parents) in the group. Why not ask a couple of students a warm-up question such as "What is one reason you're here this morning?" And a student would answer, "Because my mother made me," and everyone would laugh.

Or run some You Tube-type clips, produced by actual students? Or put out a bunch of facts, and then give students a pop quiz, with a prize for the kid who got the most correct answers (and a prize for the one who got the fewest correct answers).

She could have gone on, but luckily the presentation came to an end, and it was time to take the campus tour (which wasn't that great, either, but at least there were no PowerPoint slides).

Here are other ideas for creating a more interactive meeting:

- After a presentation, break participants into small groups (two or three people) and ask the groups to generate tough questions about the topic.
- Use an exercise called "vote with your body," in which participants move around the room to indicate their agreement with key statements.
- Put flipchart paper on the table, and invite participants to create a mind map (a diagram of related words) to brainstorm solutions to a challenge.
- Reverse the agenda for the typical town hall meeting. For the first 45 minutes of the meeting, invite employees to answer questions posed by the senior manager—to share their opinions on various topics. Then let the senior manager share what she has learned and talk about how she will use that information going forward.

Want more ideas? A slew of books are devoted to facilitating dynamic meetings. Here are three to get you started:

*How to Wow: Proven Strategies for Presenting Your Ideas, Persuading Your Audience, and Perfecting Your Image* by Frances Cole Jones (Ballantine Books, 2009)

*The Art of Facilitation* by Dale Hunter, Anne Bailey, and Bill Taylor (Jossey-Bass, 2009)

*Breaking Robert's Rules: The New Way to Run Your Meeting, Build Consensus, and Get Results* by Lawrence E. Susskind and Jeffrey L. Cruikshank (Oxford University Press, USA, 2006)

# What About Web Meetings?

Thanks to advances in technology, we no longer have to get together physically to have a meeting. We can have a teleconference, meet via videoconference, or join each other on a web meeting platform (such as Microsoft Live Meeting, Cisco Go-To-Meeting, or WebEx). The risk is that all the potential pitfalls of face-to-face meetings are magnified if you run a virtual meeting as a glorified conference call, showing PowerPoint slides but providing no opportunity to participate.

What should you do differently? Here are five ways to start:

- **Focus on your objectives.** (This is so important that we're mentioning it yet again.) Maybe you're trying to facilitate understanding among participants, or to get people to work together to solve a problem. In any case, be sure that your agenda is designed to achieve your objectives and that you're using the best web tools to support your agenda.

- **Become familiar with available features.** Many meeting organizers are uncomfortable with their video or web meeting system, so they only use the few tools they know—usually presenting PowerPoint slides. But good systems offer a wide array of tools to make meetings more dynamic. To find out what's available, watch a demo on the service's website or take the available training, which is usually free. Then begin to experiment with how you can use these features to enhance your meeting.

- **Try one new tool.**  The easiest, which is available on most web services, is Chat. It allows participants to write a question or comment, which is then posted for all to see. We use Chat to encourage participants to ask a question at any time, without interrupting the presentation. But you can use Chat in many different ways, including as a message thread.

- **Take a test drive.**  At a small team meeting, experiment with running the session completely differently, using all the options available. Instead of presenting, try the Sharing feature to show participants a sample document or website. Create a poll, and allow participants to vote. Play with the whiteboard feature. Hand over the controls to another participant, and let him or her play.

- **Trust the force.**  Virtual meetings can be a great way to communicate and get work done, if you give them a chance. So leave behind your assumptions and see what's possible.

Finally, we've found nothing beats actual face-to-face meetings for sharing information, solving problems, and more. If an international group is going to work on a project over the course of a year or many months, it's worth the investment to bring that group together for two or three days, with a mix of informal and formal get-togethers. Then, when you need to meet during the course of your project, you can do so economically via a web-based platform and have a much greater degree of participation, because participants will genuinely know each other from having had face-to-face time together.

# Support Your Local Manager

When it comes to HR communication, employees are inclined to look for answers when they need to take action or make a decision. Whom do they turn to?

Their managers, of course, who provide useful, just-in-time information.

Since most managers feel they have a business to run—and do not want to become experts in the HR field—it can be a challenge to get them to learn a bit more about HR topics. Your role is to keep managers in the loop so that they're ready to answer questions as they come up. Here are four ways to help managers succeed in this important communication role:

- **Brief managers before the rest of the organization.** When you're rolling out a new program, train managers first. They'll have the inside scoop and feel knowledgeable enough to answer questions. Hint: Our favorite (efficient) way to do this is interactive, web-based briefings.

- **Provide FAQs.** As mundane as Frequently Asked Questions are, managers find them very helpful. Don't forget to include the tough questions and avoid corporate speak. Ask real questions that employees would ask, testing your FAQs with employees and managers before you finalize them. Get rid of the jargon, and write the way you talk. The best FAQs sound like a real person (a smart one) who anticipates and answers all your questions. The worst sound like a Dilbert cartoon: great to make fun of, but of no help to managers.

- **Create an intranet microsite devoted to managers.** If your company has an intranet, consider a special section just for managers. A managers' site is perfect to house resources and build skills. Make it social by including discussion threads so that colleagues can share challenges and solutions. Provide access to on-demand learning that people can access quickly when faced with a challenge.

• **Don't ask managers to hold a special meeting.** Managers are consumed with getting the job done; they don't need more to do. Focus on helping them respond to queries as they're raised and talking about key issues in regular team meetings.

## The Five-Minute Manager

One multinational organization set up a program to send all managers a weekly e-mail with a maximum of five minutes' worth of information for the manager to share in any weekly staff meeting. By keeping to brief, highlighted information, HR made it easy for managers to do the right thing. If employees asked questions, the manager knew where to find the answers, and then he or she could share the answers with employees at the next week's staff meeting.

# Try a Meeting in a Box

There are times when you really need managers to get together with their employees on an important topic. If so, make it as easy as possible by creating a "meeting in a box." To create one, you simply combine everything a manager needs to communicate a new program into one package (which can be a physical box or an electronic download). The box will include a video overview of the new program, print handouts for employees to take away, and a discussion guide for the manager to use in a staff meeting. It can even include a feedback form to measure the usefulness of the communications. Again, if you make it easy for managers to do what you want them to do, you increase the likelihood that they will do just what you ask.

For example, let's say it's mid-year review time, and you need everyone to participate, despite the stress they're feeling right now. How? Here are three tools to give managers to encourage them to have mid-year conversations:

- **Use visuals to illustrate the process.** Create a visual map of all the steps (and who is responsible for each) to help managers understand the process.

- **Be clear about roles.** Clearly articulate the roles of both managers and employees so that everyone knows what they are expected to do.

- **Provide FAQs.** Address burning questions managers might have about the process or their role by providing them with FAQs and answers.

## Helping Managers Understand a New Compensation Plan

A pharmaceutical company revamped its variable-pay plans to create a single global program for managers called the Long-Term Incentive (LTI) Plan. The challenge was to introduce this program so that managers themselves would understand the changes and be prepared to answer questions from employees.

We created a print piece highlighting the plan's components. Then we invited managers to web-based meetings that focused on complex plan components such as restricted stock units and performance share units. The meetings were designed to present information, but a considerable amount of time was allocated for Q&A. Questions asked by managers during the sessions were collected, and at the end of all sessions, a FAQ document was created and distributed for managers to use with their employees.

As a result, 95% of managers attending the web meetings said they understood the new LTI Plan. One program—the restricted stock unit plan—required managers to take action, and 100% of those affected did so before the required deadline.

# Checklist for Making Meetings Meaningful (and Helping Managers)

✓ Start with the end in mind by creating clear, focused objectives.

✓ Build an agenda that helps create a game plan for your meeting.

✓ Create highly interactive meetings, getting everyone involved.

✓ Use PowerPoint wisely—as a visual tool, not a crutch.

✓ Make virtual meetings work better by employing available features such as chat, polls, and sharing.

✓ Brief managers so that they're comfortable with a topic and prepared to answer questions.

# 9

## Measure Effectiveness

*In this chapter, you learn how to*

- *Evaluate all dimensions of communication effectiveness*
- *Write clear survey questions*
- *Implement a survey*
- *Translate survey data into recommendations you can act on*

What's the most dangerous assumption you can make about communication? That just because you've sent a message, employees have received it, understood it, bought into it, and acted on it.

The truth is there's only one way to know your communication has been effective: by measuring its effectiveness. Measurement also helps you know how to make improvements.

That's why it's surprising that many HR and communication professionals neglect measurement. They think measurement is too time-consuming, too expensive, and too mathematical. (After all, we didn't choose our career because of our love of statistics!)

As two non-math majors, we're here to reassure you that measurement doesn't have to be difficult. In this chapter, we show you a simple model for communication measurement. We demonstrate how to apply this model to different situations. And we provide examples of survey questions and other tools, as well as advice on what *not* to do.

# Defining Effectiveness

When we started our careers, communication was considered to be more art than science. The commonly held belief was that because communication was subjective, you couldn't measure it. But we know now that effectiveness is not just a matter of preference. You can measure whether communication creates knowledge, changes minds, and influences behavior. We developed the model shown in Figure 9-1; it defines five dimensions that together equal communication effectiveness.

| Dimension | Quick definition |
|---|---|
| Action | Employees take appropriate action, as in enrolling in their health plan or completing their performance management form. |
| Belief | Communication influences employees' views; they feel the topic is credible and beneficial. |
| Understanding | Employees "get it": Information is clear and meaningful. |
| Satisfaction | Communication meets employees' needs; they find it convenient and helpful. |
| Participation | Employees access and receive communication. |

Figure 9-1    Five dimensions of communication effectiveness

How do you measure each of these? Here's an overview:

| Dimension | What Is Measured | How It's Measured |
|---|---|---|
| Action | The program's success, such as the percentage of participation and completion of a desired action | Program metrics |
| Belief | Confidence<br>Attitude<br>Credibility/trust<br>Pride | *Survey questions like this one:* The new incentive compensation plan rewards individual achievement.<br>__ Strongly agree<br>__ Agree<br>__ Disagree<br>__ Strongly disagree |
| Understanding | Knowledge of key topics<br>Understanding of actions required | *Survey questions like this one:* I know how to use the company's new travel policy.<br>__ Strongly agree<br>__ Agree<br>__ Disagree<br>__ Strongly disagree |
| Satisfaction | Relevance<br>Timeliness<br>Usefulness/value<br>Quantity and frequency<br>Ability to participate | *Survey questions like this one:* The HR portal contains useful information.<br>__ Strongly agree<br>__ Agree<br>__ Disagree<br>__ Strongly disagree |
| Participation | Open e-mails and click through to links<br>Attend meetings/sessions<br>Spend time on the intranet | Activity metrics, such as web trends data and meeting attendance |

When people think about measurement, they usually envision a survey. However, you'll notice that not every effectiveness dimension is evaluated by asking employees to complete a questionnaire. In fact, when it comes to participation and action, surveys can be deceiving: People tend to give more positive responses than their actions indicate. For example, they'll report that they visit your website several times a month, because that's what they remember. But your web metrics may indicate otherwise. Or, employees will respond that they intend to enroll in long-term disability coverage, but the only way to measure the result of that intention is through actual enrollment results.

# Survey Essentials

When you want to measure employees' beliefs, understanding, or satisfaction through a survey, here are the seven essential steps to take:

1. Create focus.
2. Choose the right method.
3. Ask good questions.
4. Get buy-in and participation.
5. Conduct the survey.
6. Analyze and report on the results.
7. Communicate and take action.

## Create Focus

If you've ever taken a survey that meanders from topic to topic, seemingly without a sense of direction, you've experienced the problem that occurs when measurement lacks focus. The survey's designers had good intentions, but somewhere along the way they lost control of the questionnaire. The result is a survey that's too expansive, making it confusing for respondents (and more likely they'll give up before they're done). Plus, because survey organizers get so much data on so many different subjects, it is difficult for them to act on all those findings.

It's much better to focus on just a few key topics and create a short survey that gives you just the results you need. To do so, start by considering your survey's purpose: the reason for the research. Purpose answers the big question: Why are we doing this survey? For example, using effectiveness dimensions as your guide, here are examples of what you might focus on:

- Satisfaction with your intranet site
- Understanding of healthcare plan choices
- Confidence that the performance management system helps employees manage their careers

## Choose the Best Method

The most commonly used research method these days is an online survey, using either web-based software or an online service such as Zoomerang or SurveyMonkey. There's good reason for this: Online surveys are cheaper, faster, and more timely. And in most cases, electronic surveys result in a greater response rate than old-fashioned paper surveys. However, before you decide to go with an online survey, consider these questions:

- **Who is your target audience?** If not all your employees have easy electronic access, by distributing a survey exclusively via e-mail or the Internet/intranet, you may overlook an important segment of your employee base. Consider using a print survey or electronic/print combination.
- **How long is your survey?** An electronic survey needs to take less time to complete than a paper survey, because it's difficult to read a computer screen for a long time. If you are planning on asking a lot of questions, an online survey isn't for you. You're much better off with a paper survey, where

employees can scan the page much more quickly. In our experience, the longer the survey, the fewer responses you'll get—so, when you want a high response rate, stick to a one-page (or one-screen) survey.

- **What is your timetable?** Electronic surveys take less time to send out, complete, and tabulate. If you're working with a tight time frame, an online survey is best.

## Ask Good Questions

The heart of every survey is questions. Writing effective survey questions is a precise science: Market researchers extensively study how people respond to words and phrases. Although you're not a research expert, you can apply the same thinking by making sure your questions are as clear and specific as possible.

Most survey questions ask about one of four attributes:

1. **What did you do? (Experiential)** Questions that ask about experiences employees have had. Opinion or belief does not play a role in answering these questions. Example: "I attended the town hall meeting last month."

2. **What do you think or believe? (Attitudinal)** Used when trying to gauge feelings, opinions, and beliefs. Example: "The benefits newsletter helps me learn about my healthcare plan choices."

3. **What do you know? (Knowledge testing)** Used when trying to gauge awareness or knowledge of an issue. Can be self-assessment or actual knowledge-testing questions. Example: "I understand how to choose the healthcare plan that's right for me."

4. **Who are you? (Demographic)** Allows you to cross-reference a person's location, tenure, job category, or other characteristics against his or her responses with results from other levels. Example: "In which region do you work? (Northeast, Midwest, Southeast, etc.)"

Whichever type of question you're writing, remember the following:

- **Be simple.**   Put away your thesaurus, and forget all the fancy words you know.
- **Know precisely what you're asking.**   Ill-defined or vague questions are an easy trap. You may understand what you mean by a question such as "Do you believe you have enough information to support our strategies?", but will your respondent? What exactly is "support?"
- **Include only one concept.**   Keep your questions narrowly focused. Two questions combined into one create confusion. For example, if you ask employees about their level of agreement with the statement "E-mails from HR and Employee Communication are timely," you're really asking two questions. While you may be interested in e-mails generally, employees may have different experiences with the two distinct sources.
- **Avoid jargon or obscure language.**   Don't use complex terms the participant might be unfamiliar with.
- **Stay neutral.**   Make sure you avoid leading questions that can influence a participant to a certain response. Leading questions are a common problem that violates the integrity of your data. How could an employee disagree with "I am actively involved in setting my goals and objectives" or "I never have enough time to take advantage of career development courses"?
- **Use a consistent four-point scale.**   There's a lot of debate in the research world about which answer scale is best. A 5-point scale, from "strongly agree" to "strongly disagree" with "neutral" in the middle? A scale that varies from question to question? For more complex topics, a 7- or even 10-point scale? Here's what we've found works best. Create a simple 4-point scale—Strongly Agree, Agree, Disagree, Strongly Disagree—and design all your questions as statements ("The open enrollment package answers all my questions about healthcare plans"). Eliminate the middle "Neutral" response; for most communication questions you ask, employees have a distinct opinion and don't need the Neutral option. Use the same scale throughout your survey for consistency.

- **Limit open-ended questions.** Too many open-ended or write-in questions will contribute to a condition called "Survey Shutdown," in which a respondent leaves the survey before he or she is finished. Every survey should be limited to one open-ended question. If you feel the need to include many open-ended questions, a focus group is the better option.

*(Bad) Example: Survey Fatigue*

One of the professional organizations that Alison belongs to conducted a survey about the organization's print publication and its electronic newsletter. Since Alison believes that feedback is a good thing, she decided to participate.

But the survey was so long, extensive, and open-ended that it was exhausting to complete. It contained 29 questions, a lot for an online survey. Even worse, 16 of those questions were open-ended. And they weren't the usual "Do you have any suggestions?" questions; they required deep thought. Here are just a few examples:

- "List up to five issues or trends in branding and marketing that you want us to address in our magazine."
- "What do you like best about our magazine?"
- "What other industry-related e-newsletters do you subscribe to?
- "What kinds of products or services would you like to see advertised in our magazine or e-newsletter?"

Whew! Only the most dedicated reader (or member) would take the time to answer every question. Most people would either do what Alison did—answer just a few questions and skip the others—or get to a certain point and jump ship. In research parlance, that's called "noncompletion."

What caused this problem? There are at least two reasons. First, the survey creators wanted to explore issues in an open-ended way. But the wrong tool for this job is a survey, which is a quantitative, closed-ended, data-producing instrument. The right method is qualitative—either focus groups or interviews.

Second, the creators didn't consider the experience of survey respondents. If the creators had tested the survey, they would have realized that completing it would take at least 15 and probably up to 30 minutes—way too long for an online survey.

Before you are tempted to include open-ended questions in your next survey, consider the fatigue factor.

## *Get Buy-in and Participation*

Preparing the organization to participate in your survey requires as much effort as developing the right set of questions. If you conduct research without adequate communication in advance, your target audience may fail to see its value, which may negatively impact participation.

Depending on the breadth of your survey, you should reach out to three primary audiences:

- **Senior leaders.** It's important to engage this group, because you may be knocking on their doors when you have your results and recommendations in hand. Be sure they understand how you intend to help the business with the results. And if you have any expectations about their role, such as encouraging participation, be explicit. You should also explain how results will be shared (and expectations about their use).
- **Managers.** Requesting information from employees usually means that managers will get questions. Be sure this group understands the timeline, what you want to accomplish, how employees will be invited, and what you want them to do. Then they'll be ready for questions.
- **Employees.** Use a variety of channels to remind employees of upcoming research (e-mail, print, bulletin board posting, staff meetings, voice mail, newsletter article). Hearing about research many times and in different ways will make employees more aware of it.

For all these stakeholders, here are the points you should cover as you set expectations about your upcoming survey:

- **Purpose:** The reason for the research and what you're trying to accomplish.
- **Topics:** The main areas of your research.
- **Logistics:** The target participants and why, as well as who is running the survey.
- **Methodology:** How the survey will be distributed.
- **Results:** What will be done with findings and how changes or actions will be decided.
- **Timeline:** When the research begins and when results will be shared.
- **Benefit:** Why input is important and what's in it for participants.

## Conduct the Survey

Asking the right questions won't be as valuable if you don't ask the right people to participate. That's why it's important to think carefully about your "sample" or selection of participants.

Start by defining your overall target population. Are you looking to study the entire company? A specific site or division? Certain types of employees, such as hourly workers? This first selection is your "target sample" or universe of participants.

Your next step is determining your sample. The most commonly used methods of sampling are a census (your entire organization) or a random sample (a representative group in your organization).

Use a census survey when you want to include everyone in your target sample or your entire organization. A census survey is simple—just ask everyone to participate—and it signals that every opinion matters. However, if your organization is large or complex, a census may be logistically difficult and expensive. And when people in an organization always ask everyone to participate in every survey, employees may begin feeling over-researched.

That's why you should consider a random sample. This is a statistically valid way to conduct research that is routinely used by professional polling companies. For example, when campaigns want to learn what U.S. voters will do, they use random sampling to choose 1,000 people who will represent the entire electorate. In your company, use a random sample as a cost-effective method for taking the pulse of your organization. By systematically choosing names from your employee database (a common method is to select every 11th name), you can be assured of viewpoints that are representative of the entire employee population.

### Delivering the Survey

After you've set your sample, you're ready to survey. Here are tips for managing the process:

- Provide detailed instructions, along with contact information. This will help people if they have trouble with the survey form.
- For print surveys, provide an envelope for easy return.
- Be up front about how long it will take to answer the survey, especially if it takes people away from their jobs.
- Communicate the deadline for the survey to be returned. Don't allow too much time, since people tend to answer surveys shortly after receiving them.
- For online surveys, don't include too many questions on one page. If you're using multiple web page screens, let people know how many questions they have left to answer.

### Analyze and Report on the Results

The results are in! Now you must tabulate the numbers and figure out what they mean and what to do about them. We recommend taking your time to understand fully what the feedback is telling you:

- Start by reviewing the purpose and focus of your survey. Remind yourself what you set out to learn, and keep that top of mind while you analyze the results.

- Now look at the raw data for each question. If your software translates these numbers into percentages, that saves you a step; if not, use your calculator (or a friend in finance) to figure out percentages for each response.

- Begin to draw conclusions. We've found that the best way to do so is to collaborate with one or more colleagues. Give each team member a copy of the raw data report to review, and then get together in a spacious conference room. Using large Post-it Notes, ask each member to record findings, one per Post-it, that seem significant. Group trends, and discuss what the results are telling you. Discuss which results met your expectations and which did not.

- Look for separate results from individual questions that work together to tell a story. For example, you may have asked a question about how helpful your intranet site is for finding information about healthcare plan choices. Another question may have asked how well employees understand a new plan choice. By comparing the results of both questions, you begin to tell a story about how well communication is working to create understanding about healthcare.

- Organize open-ended comments by topic. Use those comments to add texture to your quantitative findings.

- Create five to seven key findings, the main conclusions of your survey results. Decide what you will do in response; these actions become your recommendations.

## Creating a Research Report

Based on your analysis, create a report in PowerPoint or Word that includes the following:

- **Introduction:** States the survey's purpose.
- **Methodology:** Addresses how the survey was conducted, including these elements:
  - Timing
  - Sample or census
  - How the results compare to previous surveys, if applicable
- **Key findings:** Summarizes overriding themes.
- **Detailed findings:** Focuses on details, including results for each question.
- **Recommendations:** Provides action steps and answers the questions "What should we do to move forward?" and "What is the next step we should take?"

### *Communicate and Take Action*

Here's a step that's often overlooked: communicating results to key stakeholders, including employees who took the time to participate. Start by sharing the results with leaders so that you can get buy-in for making changes. For example, suppose your results point to the need for more tools to help managers communicate. You need to create a clear picture of how the data supports this need—from preferences to the current effectiveness of manager communication. You also need to demonstrate potential impact on the business, such as better engagement.

Employees need confirmation that you take their feedback seriously. Not only does this signal that the organization is listening, but it also encourages future participation. With most surveys, it can take time to agree on the next steps, especially if a large investment or major change is involved. Plan to share two or three key findings, as well as where you are in the process, within three to four weeks of the survey. Also pledge to keep the lines of communication open as you move forward.

## A Benefits Survey

Several years ago, the benefits team at a leading pharmaceutical company sought to learn about employee perceptions about their benefits, and how well employees' communication needs were being met.

The team sent a survey request to a sample of 8,000 employees (out of 60,000); 5,000 completed the survey, for a response rate of 63%. Although most employees completed a web-based survey, the team wanted to make sure that manufacturing employees were included, so paper surveys were distributed at two company plants.

Here were the survey's key findings:

- Employees felt most informed about vacation, prescription drug, and 401(k) benefits, and less informed about pension, the PPO, the HMO, and long-term disability.
- Employees felt better informed about dental and prescription drug benefits than about any of the individual medical plans.
- Sixty-six percent of employees agreed that the company "gives me enough information to make informed benefits decisions."
- Most find web technology convenient for benefit transactions, but they would like to rely less on the intranet for benefits information.

The benefits team concluded that there was great potential for improving understanding of key benefits by designing communication that better met employees' needs. The team developed a communication program for open enrollment that included a mail-to-home enrollment package. It gave details of benefits employees knew less about and included a schedule of health fairs with booths staffed by managers of targeted programs, including pension and long-term disability.

# Checklist for Measuring Communication Effectiveness

✓ Consider five dimensions—participation, satisfaction, under-standing, belief, and action—when measuring communication effectiveness.

✓ Focus your survey on just a few key areas you can act upon.

✓ Make survey questions clear and concrete.

✓ Communicate the purpose of your research to encourage buy-in.

✓ Consider a sample instead of asking all employees to partici-pate.

✓ Analyze your findings by taking the time to draw conclusions and look for patterns.

✓ Share the results of your survey as well as action steps you intend to take.

# Part II

## Communicating in Key Situations

# 10

## Recruiting

*In this chapter, you learn how to create effective recruiting communication by*

- *Describing your company's culture in a compelling way*
- *Using real employees to tell your company story*
- *Providing candidates with easy-to-access information about benefits*
- *Using the right mix of communication channels to reach every promising candidate*

## "We Want Only the Best and Brightest"

Firms that want to acquire talented people typically say they want to hire "the best and brightest." Let's step back for a moment and ask what that really means.

The best person to fill the bill in *your* company may not rank anywhere near the "brightest" in *my* company. For every organization looking for creative people, even more firms are seeking methodical, detail-oriented workers. Many companies have talent needs in between the left-brain/right-brain spectrum. Our point is that there's no right or wrong here—only the appropriate hire for your organization.

In fact, if your organization is large, many "right answers" might describe candidates; the same qualities and work ethic that lead to success in one business might not translate well into another.

Given the high cost of failure when an employee doesn't work out, your company needs to invest the time and energy up front to find people with the knowledge, experience, and expertise to succeed. And these people need to fit the culture of your company. Through both the recruiting and onboarding processes (see Chapter 11, "Orientation"), talented people need to know what it's like to work at your company before they start. After they join, they need coaching, mentoring, information, and feedback to ensure that they'll succeed.

# Keys to Successful Recruiting Communications

Here are five steps you can take to make sure your communication helps your firm acquire the talent you need:

1. Present a clear portrait of your company and its culture.
2. Feature employees describing their jobs and "what it's like to work here."
3. Create job descriptions that accurately describe what the candidate will do every day.
4. Give candidates a thorough overview of company benefits.
5. Use the right tool for the job in recruiting communication.

Let's take a more detailed look at how you can accomplish these goals.

## What It Costs to Bring in a Bad Fit

If you research the cost of employee turnover, you'll see most estimates start at about 150% of salary and increase up to 250% for leaders, people with special or highly valued skills, and senior sales professionals.

## Present a Clear Portrait of Your Company

Let's start with a "don't": As tempting as it might be, don't oversell what your company represents or offers. Presenting your organization in a warmer glow than it deserves does not serve you well. It means people might be attracted to your firm and then become unhappy once they start work.

We find it helpful to think about the recruiting process as providing information to potential candidates so that they can opt in or opt out. Either way, that's good for your company. If there's something about your company that really excites a candidate, that person will apply. Conversely, if there's something that prevents someone from even wanting to meet with you to know more, you probably don't want to waste time and talent trying to persuade that person to join you.

### Define Your Culture

Allan A. Kennedy and Terrence E. Deal coauthored *Corporate Cultures: The Rites and Rituals of Corporate Life*. A former McKinsey consultant, Kennedy likes to define "company culture" as a fancy way of saying, "That's how we do things around here."[1]

Deal and Kennedy point out that a strong culture is a powerful lever for guiding behavior and helps employees do their jobs better in a couple ways. Specifically, a strong culture

- Serves as a system of informal rules that spells out how people should behave most of the time
- Helps people feel better about the work they do, so they are more likely to work harder

The authors point out that there's no "one size fits all" corporate culture. Indeed, they note that the corporate cultures at GE and Xerox were so different in the 1980s that even though both companies were highly successful, the chances that a rising star at GE would or could replicate that success at Xerox were slim to none.

## Articulate Who You Are

After you've thought about what your company truly stands for, articulate this in a straightforward and descriptive way. To demonstrate, here are excerpts from two "who we are" descriptions from two very different companies:

- **FedEx.** "The core philosophy that governs every activity at FedEx is People-Service-Profit (PSP): Take care of our people; they in turn will deliver impeccable service demanded by our customers, who will reward us with the profitability necessary to secure our future. People-Service-Profit: These three words are the very foundation of FedEx. FedEx is dedicated to the principle that our people are our most important asset—a belief that motivated and conscientious people provide necessary professional service to ensure profits and continued growth."

- **Procter & Gamble.** "At P&G, it's about integrity and character. It's about building trust by being open, honest, straightforward, and candid with each other, our customers, consumers, and business partners. We do what we say, and we say what we mean. This is what sets P&G and P&G people apart. As a 'build from within' organization, we see 95% of our people start at entry level and then progress and prosper throughout the organization. This not only creates many wonderful opportunities to grow and advance, it creates a special camaraderie among fellow P&Gers, many of whom came up through the ranks together."

## Feature Your Employees Describing Their Jobs

To describe your company and "what it's like to work here" accurately and positively, we've found what works best are photos and video clips of, and quotes from, real employees.

You'll want to feature people with backgrounds (education, experiences) you want to replicate. If you want former Peace Corps members in your organization, always feature one in your recruiting communications. People like to see "Here's someone just like me," because it gives them confidence that this is an organization where their degrees, experience, or education will be valued. And they can see this is a place where they potentially will fit in.

How do you get employees to tell you in their own words what they like about being at your company? Ask them. Here are the types of questions that will give you great information to use in recruiting communications:

- What attracted you to this job? Does the reality of the job live up to your expectations?
- What do you like *best* about your job, and why?
- What do you like *least* about your job, and why?
- Tell me about your typical day at work—and pretend you're talking to a 12-year-old. (Adding the part about the 12-year-old helps the employee describe his or her day without using a lot of jargon.)
- What are you learning on the job?
- What skills and abilities do you need to succeed in this job?
- What is the next step you'd like to take in your career? How is your current job preparing you for your next career move?
- What advice would you offer a friend about joining this organization?
- What advice would you offer a friend about how to succeed here?
- What makes you proud of your company?

We've found that we can ask this set of questions of selected employees throughout the world and get lots of useable quotes in return. In one global financial institution, Jane posed these questions to 25 employees. Most agreed that "the work we do and the people we work with" were what employees liked best about the job.

In fact, as we've worked on recruiting communications through the years, we've realized that describing "the work you'll do and the people you'll work with" should constitute the core of every organization's recruiting communications.

## Google, Our Role Model

Most HR professionals we know have a love/hate relationship with Google. Sure, the company exemplifies "Best Place to Work," but Google is so much thinner, prettier, and richer than most of our organizations that it's hard to relate to. (If life is like high school, it's the difference between the homecoming queen and the rest of us.)

However, we like to watch what Google does and see if we can learn from it. And in recruiting communication, there's a lot to learn.

Start with the headline on Google's website section that covers employment. It reads: "Let's work together." The site features brief videos of real employees and job descriptions that make sense. There's an overview of the Google selection process, which is thorough, because the company wants to hire only people it believes will succeed.

We also like how the company describes its "Top 10 reasons to work for Google," including the following:

- **Life is beautiful.** Being a part of something that matters and working on products in which you can believe is remarkably fulfilling.

- **Appreciation is the best motivation**, so we've created a fun and inspiring workspace you'll be glad to be a part of, including on-site doctor and dentist; massage and yoga; professional development opportunities; shoreline running trails; and plenty of snacks to get you through the day.

- **Work and play are not mutually exclusive.** It is possible to code and pass the puck at the same time.

- **We love our employees, and we want them to know it.** Google offers a variety of benefits, including a choice of medical programs, company-matched 401(k), stock options, maternity and paternity leave, and much more.

*How Quotes from Employees Add Value*

As you interview employees for your recruiting communications, you'll hear wonderful examples and expressions of your company's culture, job content, and more. Here are examples from some of Jane's recruiting communication efforts:

- "Each new job I've accepted didn't exist before I took it" (from the then-Chairman).
- "This business takes aggressiveness, because we often have to try 10 different strategies in order to succeed at one."
- "You have to love numbers and be very detail-oriented. You can't breeze through financial reports."
- "Creativity is important in anticipating problems before they occur and resolving them when they crop up unexpectedly."
- "To succeed here, you have to be aggressive, to spot opportunities and take advantage of them. Then, you work with a team of people to get the job done."
- "We're driven to be much more innovative here, and I like that pressure."

## John Deere Profiles

The power equipment company John Deere uses a simple technique to feature its employees on the recruiting section of its website. Along the top are 17 thumbnail photos of representative employees. Click any of these and you're introduced to an employee. Here, for example, is Matt, a cost accountant at the Des Moines Works in Ankeny, Iowa. Matt is clearly young, somewhat hip (nice hair, Matt!), and friendly (great smile, too!).

Here are some of the thoughts Matt shares about his job and the company:

- "They backed me up 100%. I have a bachelor's in accounting and also received my CPA license. John Deere backed me up 100% and helped me pay for the tests and license fee."

*continued*

- "Choose your best fit. John Deere hired me into the accounting department on the FDP (Finance Development Program) rotation. The FDP is a three-year program where you rotate to a new position each year... Rotation provides the opportunity to choose the area that best fits your skills and interests."
- "It's all about the atmosphere. The company is a close-knit community, and everyone finds time to have fun while still being productive. People are so friendly. Maybe it's just the Iowa atmosphere."

## Create Accurate Job Descriptions

How does a candidate know if he or she really wants the job? From the job description, which paints a picture of what the candidate will be doing every day at work.

The key is to put the legal, technical description back in your personnel files and instead create a description that speaks to the candidate.

As an example of what not to do, here's an excerpt from a description that has been slightly altered to protect the guilty:

We're looking for a business/marketing expert who is a strategic and creative thinker with a natural ability to translate complex technical concepts into business results-oriented narratives that resonate with the organization, business, and industry. You will develop and drive a group-wide communication plan that ensures message clarity and consistency through every level of the organization. The communication plan will clearly establish the communication rhythm of the business (ROB) for your senior leaders and will align with the overall Company ROB calendar. You will work closely with senior leaders to ensure that their communications (i.e., executive newsletters, e-mails, presentations, etc.) to the organization, business, and industry have powerful impact and are carried out flawlessly. You will be on point to ensure that content, deliverables, demos, and supporting materials are compelling, consistent with other executives' communications, and reinforce the Company story and value proposition to the organization, business, and industry.

Can't you just picture a Dilbert-like person returning home from this job, opening the door, and saying: "Honey, I'm home. Today I drove process improvement. Tomorrow, I hope to display my natural ability to translate complex technical concepts into business results-oriented narratives that resonate with . . . Honey?"

This job description contains more jargon than information and doesn't convey what expertise is needed to do the job. It doesn't answer these questions: What's the level of responsibility: strategic or tactical? What will the person in this job learn? What could this job lead to?

## The J.M. Smucker Company

By contrast, we like how the jam company Smucker's writes its job descriptions. (We like how the company makes jam, too, but that's a different story.) Here's part of a description of an assistant manager for the consumer communications center. What we like is how specific the description is. We'd like it to be a bit more inspirational, but we appreciate that a candidate would know exactly what the job is all about:

**Location:** Orrville, Ohio

**Reports to:** Manager, Consumer Communications Center

**Job scope:** This position is responsible primarily for assisting the Consumer Communications Center Manager in the development of Consumer Communications Representatives through coaching, training, supporting, and career development. In addition, this position is responsible for supporting the performance goals of the operation, including consumer-escalated situations, managing systems, and maintaining levels of service.

**Key responsibilities:**

• Develop/support the consumer communications representative.

*continued*

- Provide motivation and maintain high levels of morale in a call center environment.

- Conduct monthly employee reviews utilizing ACD statistics, ePC results, and quality audits on call observations and data-entry accuracy.

- Mediate conflicts within the team and with individuals and groups that support the consumer communications center.

- Handle employee relations/performance issues as they arise.

- Handle escalated consumer contacts while modeling the behaviors and skills required for handling escalated contacts.

- Review follow-up completed by the representative to ensure what was promised was delivered.

## Give Candidates a Thorough Overview of Company Benefits

Your company has a full set of benefits and policies meant to retain your most valuable employees. But you may forget that any one of those benefits may create a compelling reason for a potential hire to submit his application. We've found that different benefits matter more to different candidates, based on their situation. That's why you should make sure that your full spectrum of benefits and policies is easily accessible in your recruiting communication.

For example, Monsanto's recruiting website contains a section called "Helping busy people living busy lives." It includes a "high-level overview of the benefit plans Monsanto offers to eligible employees." It contains links to sections on medical, vision, and life insurance benefits; pension and stock purchase plans; and time off and other key policies.

Although the information is certainly not as comprehensive as a Summary Plan Description, it provides enough details to give you a sense of what Monsanto offers. For example, here is an excerpt from the Dental Plan section:

### Two Levels of Benefits

The Dental Plan is designed to help pay the expenses of dental care. Two levels of dental benefits are offered: high and low.

Under the high option, a covered individual can receive benefits up to $2,000 each year. The low option provides up to $1,500 each year. There is a separate orthodontia lifetime maximum of $1,650 per covered individual under the high option—$1,250 per covered individual under the low option.

If you use an out-of-network provider, you will be responsible for any amounts that exceed the maximum amount allowed in the area as well as your out-of-network deductible and co-pays.

## *Use the Right Tool in Recruiting Communication*

No doubt you're aware that the hottest trend in recruitment communication can be summed up in two words: social media. More companies every day are getting involved in such social networks as LinkedIn and Facebook, are posting videos on YouTube, or are sharing job openings or other information (very briefly) through the microblog Twitter.

We believe that these new communication channels offer valuable ways to connect with job candidates. But social media is not the answer to everything. As mentioned in Chapter 7, "Use the Right Tool for the Job," you still need a mix of tools—and an understanding of which works best for which purpose—to reach your future employees.

Here are a few things to remember when using social media tools in recruitment communication:

- **Be short and sweet.** Twitter posts, or "tweets," are limited to 140 characters, and there's an expectation that all content will be quick and timely. For example, here are some tweets that were posted on the Raytheon job site:

"Program Manager position opening at Raytheon in Arlington, VA."

"Data Center Network Specialist job opening at Raytheon in Rosslyn, VA."

"Pre-register for Raytheon's HW/SW Invitational in Denver (July 14 and 15)."

- **Coordinate your efforts.** Some candidates may love the update experience of Twitter, others may be Facebook fanatics, and still others may limit their job search to surfing the web. Make sure that the most important information you want to convey is accessible in all channels, including more traditional venues such as job websites.

- **Get employees involved.** As we mentioned early in this chapter, employee faces and voices are more convincing than any message that "the company" conveys. And this is especially true in social media, which is, after all, a social communication channel. Recruiting teams at companies such as Deloitte, Hewlett Packard, and even the U.S. Army have learned to stay in the background while shining the spotlight on employees. Candidates can direct questions to employees, creating confidence that they're getting the straight story. That's powerful stuff.

## Using Video Clips to Acquire Hard-to-Get Talent

A global pharmaceutical firm was growing quickly and needed to hire several hundred employees around the world in all parts of the business. The company's solution was to tap into the passion of current employees and jump into social media at the same time. They asked employees to turn the camera on themselves and say why they worked there (the good, the bad, and the ugly). The company held an internal contest where employees voted on their favorite videos and then pushed the "employee-generated content" externally (through Facebook, Google, and so on) to attract new hires.

To achieve this, the company sent 125 FLIP video cameras to all locations and relied on the site head administrative assistants to manage the "lending library" of cameras. (Generally, they provided one camera for every 50 employees.) The program was voluntary, and the company received 132 submissions from 28 countries. "It was really a fun campaign," says the lead communicator. "And while this program wasn't the only key to our success, it was an important element, and we achieved our hiring goals."

# Checklist for Recruiting Talent

If you're serious about attracting the best people for your company, here are some suggestions to help you communicate effectively:

✓ Check out the employment sections of the websites of companies you admire. Compare what they offer and how they present their employment proposition with how your company does it. What can you do differently to improve your talent acquisition communications?

✓ Let real employees do the talking—and feature people you want to replicate in your new recruits. Don't limit yourself to a "one of each" approach to diversity (one white, one black, one . . .)—it's really dated.

✓ If your company takes months to make a decision, let new hires know that; don't sugarcoat parts of your company culture you think may not appeal to potential employees. When a new employee leaves after a short time, it's a lose-lose situation that costs your company time and money.

# 11

## Orientation

*In this chapter, you learn how to help new employees feel knowledgeable about the company so they're prepared to do great work. We share advice on how to*

- *Help managers understand their role in orientation and give them the tools they need to succeed*
- *Build an effective orientation process*
- *Create an orientation session that informs and inspires*

## Welcome Aboard!

The good news is that you've just hired a terrific person for that open position. The bad news is that there's a good chance your new employee might not work out. In fact, according to a study by the training company Leadership IQ, only 19% of new hires achieve unequivocal success within their first 18 months on the job.

What can you do to increase your odds? Build an effective orientation process and program. Traditionally, HR managers focus on the **orientation session**, which we define as the formal event that employees attend (either in person or virtually) to learn essential information about the company.

But, although that program is vitally important, it's not enough to ensure that new employees are set up for success. For that, you need to develop a more holistic **orientation process** that is well understood by managers and employees. (Some companies call this process "onboarding," as in "getting the new hire on board.")

This process is critical because orientation isn't a one-day experience; it occurs over time, beginning when a person is hired and ending when that person is completely performing the job he or she was hired to do:

- For some positions, the process of orientation may take less than a day, because the new hire can begin performing his or her job duties successfully right from the start.
- For more senior-level employees with specific expertise or experience, the process can take much longer (six months to a year, for example) and requires a bit more effort (but it's more than worth the effort, we must add).

In this chapter, we focus on the communication components of orientation: briefing managers, building an orientation process, and holding an orientation session.

# Before You Begin

We've spent a lot of time listening to employees over the years—both those who just started at their companies, and those who have been around a while. That's how we know that new employees in particular want answers to a universal set of questions. If you keep these questions in mind when designing your orientation process, you'll give employees the answers they seek:

- What business is our company in, and how do we stack up against the competition?
- What's our company history?
- What is our company mission (why we exist) and vision (where we're headed)?
- Who's in charge? What's our current business structure, and who are the people on our management team?

- Why should I care about all these points? What's in it for me?
- How can I succeed here?

Like every communication project, creating an effective orientation program starts with **research**. We've found that the best research for this purpose is qualitative, which means conducting an open-ended dialog with people. Here are some techniques you might try:

- Ask HR professionals from various businesses or locations in your company what information new hires need to succeed.
- Find out some of the reasons people gave in exit interviews for leaving the company within the first year.
- Conduct a focus group with successful people in your company to find out which experiences and information helped them most when they were new to the firm.
- Interview senior managers and find out what they want every new person to know about the company and how it's important to the company's success.
- Talk with representatives of key functions (Marketing, IT, Legal, for example) to find out what they want new hires to know about their area.

Based on your research, set goals for your process and program, and then develop content and delivery and determine how you'll get feedback.

## "My First Week"

As you explore improving your orientation process, here's a great question to ask: "What do you remember most about your first day or week?" Alison's firm recently asked this of a team of employees on an onboarding project and heard the good, bad, and ugly of their orientation experiences. Here is some of what they told us:

- "I didn't get my computer on the first day, so I couldn't really do any work."

- "My cubicle was completely ready for me: computer, office supplies, working phone, etc. That made me feel as if my department wanted me to be there."

- "My manager arranged meetings with key people during my first two weeks on the job. Those meetings were so valuable for getting up to speed and building relationships with people who would be critical to my success."

- "I was brought into a conference room and given a stack of HR documents to read, and forms to sign. I thought, 'I'll never absorb all this, so I'll have to ask my colleagues questions later.'"

- "I had moved between the time I accepted the job and my first day at work, so I needed to fill out a change-of-address online form for payroll. It took me two hours to find the form and figure out how to fill it out."

- "I had a welcoming committee! The whole team greeted me at the front door and took me to my office. At lunchtime, my boss ordered pizza for everyone. By the end of the day, I felt like I knew my coworkers pretty well."

# Set Up Managers for Success

If yours is like most organizations, your research will reveal that the single most important person in the orientation process is the new employee's manager. Even if your company has a well-integrated onboarding system in place—involving HR, facilities, IT, and other functions—the manager is the glue that holds it all together. For example, the manager does the following:

- Works with other groups to make sure the new employee receives the basics: a space in which to work, a phone, a computer, a company ID, and so on.

- Helps the employee understand what he can expect of the company and what the company expects of him.

- Introduces the new hire to the people inside and outside the department that he will work with. (Because of the collaborative nature of most work, it's important that the new hire begin meeting with the people who will be important to his or her success starting on the first day.)

- Sends an e-mail to colleagues the new hire will be working with that gives an overview of the new hire's work experience, skills, and expertise—and perhaps a fun fact or two. The idea is to give new colleagues some conversation starters as they meet the new hire.

- Provides meaningful work that the employee can do right away and gives feedback so that the work gets done properly.

- Sets goals and provides coaching to help the new employee succeed.

Your job is to make it easy for the manager to provide an effective orientation. This starts with articulating the manager's role. Don't assume that just because the manager participated in recruiting, he will understand what's expected of him as soon as the new employee starts the job.

## "What Should We Be Doing?"

We recently conducted interviews and focus groups at a global industrial company to determine how the orientation process was working and to guide the development of new materials to support orientation. We spoke to local HR representatives, managers, and recently hired employees. Here's what we learned:

- HR reps believed that orientation is the managers' responsibility. "But managers don't know it's their job," said one HR rep, "so we end up filling in the gaps."

- Managers knew they should be involved in orientation but were unclear what to do. Managers who routinely bring new employees on board were much more comfortable with the orientation process than managers who only occasionally hire a new person.

- All the managers we talked to requested a "playbook." "I'd like to understand exactly how the process is supposed to

*continued*

work, and have all the tools available when I need them," said a manager.

- New employees appreciated any help they could get. "Starting a new job is an overwhelming experience," said a newly hired engineer. "Every moment my manager spends with me is very valuable. But I know my manager is busy, so I appreciate tools like online training, a website, and background materials."

Our recommendation? That the company focus not only on creating orientation tools and resources, but it also needs to define roles more clearly for HR, managers, and employees so that everyone understands what's expected of them.

# Translate the Manager's Role into Action

When we refer to defining a manager's role, we don't mean creating a long, detailed document with lots of bullet points. Managers are action-oriented. Their big question is, "What do I need to do?" (They very seldom ask the existential Hamlet question, "To be, or not to be?") So, as we heard at the industrial company, managers want a "playbook"—a guide to the steps involved in orienting a new employee—with the supporting tools and information that will help them take those steps.

We find that, since managers live by their calendar, the best way to provide this information is within a timeline. After all, the process of orientation starts on the first day and ends when the new employee is fully performing on the job. So managers need to know what must happen when.

The timeline should cover the entire orientation process and describe all the things that need to happen during that process.

Figure 11-1 is a partial example of what you might include.

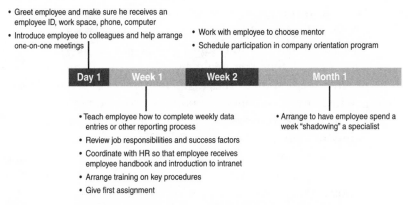

- Greet employee and make sure he receives an employee ID, work space, phone, computer
- Introduce employee to colleagues and help arrange one-on-one meetings
- Work with employee to choose mentor
- Schedule participation in company orientation program

| Day 1 | Week 1 | Week 2 | Month 1 |

- Teach employee how to complete weekly data entries or other reporting process
- Review job responsibilities and success factors
- Coordinate with HR so that employee receives employee handbook and introduction to intranet
- Arrange training on key procedures
- Give first assignment
- Arrange to have employee spend a week "shadowing" a specialist

**Figure 11-1    Manager's timeline for employee orientation**

# That Special Day: The Orientation Program

An orientation program is hardly a new concept. After all, for almost as long as companies have existed, HR departments have been inviting new employees to spend a day (or more) learning about the organization and its products or services, meeting senior leaders, and finding out "how we do things here."

But just because orientation programs have been around a while doesn't mean there aren't ways to make them more effective. Here are five ways smart companies are breathing new energy into orientation programs:

- **Have a clear idea (yes, an objective) of what you need the orientation program to accomplish.** Is the emphasis on company knowledge? Engaging new employees in the culture (which can be defined as how we work together)? Understanding how their job fits into the strategy? Decide on a few focus areas, and handle other activities differently.

- **Don't treat the orientation program as a catchall for everything a new employee needs to know or do.** The new employee has to fill out forms, for example, but that activity can be handled another time—even before the first day of work.

- **Give new employees a chance to interact with each other.** If you want to break down the silos that insulate some business units from others and give people a chance to get to know one another, you might schedule a couple of orientation programs a year and bring together employees from different geographies. If it's more important to get employees up to speed quickly, you may hold more frequent orientation programs in different locations. In either case, make sure you include "getting to know you" time in your agenda. Building good relationships with colleagues right from the start is an important step toward success for both the new employee and the company.

- **Think about the advantages and disadvantages of "going virtual."** After all, with today's online learning and web/videoconferencing meetings, you don't need a physical orientation program to cover some of what new employees need to know. So you may choose to make part of your orientation program a virtual experience. While it may be tempting to create an orientation section on your website and check off "orientation process" from your to-do list, please don't. Some of the most important advice a new hire receives will come from personal conversations, not by clicking one link after another. Again, research will help you determine what information will work best online and which needs to be in person.

- **Break open the traditional boring agenda.** If new employees have to sit still in their seats all day, listening to people lecture and watching PowerPoint, they won't be jazzed about your organization. You've made a big investment in hiring these new employees and bringing them together. An orientation session shouldn't be a passive activity; it should be a motivating, participative experience.

# A New Format for Your Orientation Program

How do you break the bounds of PowerPoint? Begin with the premise that you are there to engage employees in learning about a few key topics, not to cram information into their heads the way you stuff a Thanksgiving turkey! (By the way, we prefer cornbread with sausage.)

You can't eliminate presentations; after all, they are a proven way to share information. But you can make the program more interactive and energetic by designing sessions that involve participants and let them explore as well as listen:

| Questions | Possible Action |
|---|---|
| What business is our company in, and how do we stack up against the competition? | Make it a game with "valuable prizes" (such as company logo apparel or gift cards to local lunch joints). Two formats that work well: Jeopardy or a cyber scavenger hunt, where you pit teams against each other as they search for information on the intranet and Internet. |
| Where is our company headed? Who's in charge? What's our current business structure, and who are the people on our management team? | Invite a senior manager to be a guest. Ask the manager not only to do a standard presentation, but also to share personal stories about "my first day at the company" and "five lessons I've learned about succeeding here." Challenge new employees to come up with the toughest question they can think of, and encourage the senior manager to give a prize for the best question. |
| What are our company values? | Invite three to five "real" employees at various levels to lead breakout groups. In each group, present scenarios that explore a value, and ask new employees to address the challenge presented. Share solutions with the entire group. |
| How can I succeed here? | This is another great opportunity to bring in current employees to share their stories. Schedule a web meeting/conference call with employees across the company, set up like a radio talk show with you as the host. Make sure that employees are prepared by giving them the questions in advance. Ask, "What characteristics make people successful? What challenges have you faced, and how have you dealt with them?" Be sure to cover the ugly counterpart to this question, "What will get me fired?", so that new hires understand both success and failure at the company in clear, precise terms. |

# Fun Facts

When Jane hosted an orientation program one year, she started the day by giving the audience some positive feedback—a technique you might find helpful in your next orientation program. She said:

> "To give you an idea of how special you are, I'd like to share with you a few statistics about our recruiting process. Each year, we interview at 62 colleges in the U.S. Each year, the management recruiting office here in New York receives more than 15,000 resumes from people who want the jobs you have. Typically, we interview 14 people for every one person who's hired. By the end of this year, we'll hire 1,300 new professionals worldwide—900 of those in the U.S. And we'll hire 600 management associates worldwide—300 of those in the U.S. More than 50% of the new management associates and professionals we hire have graduate degrees."

## Example: ZS Associates Invests in New Employees

We'd like to introduce you to a company that has made a serious commitment to its orientation program: ZS Associates, a consulting firm specializing in sales and marketing consulting and outsourcing, with more than 1,500 employees working in 20 offices around the world.

When ZS was founded in the early 1980s, it was easy to bring new employees on board, since everyone worked in the same office and interacted daily with the company founders. But as the company grew, it became clear that a special effort was needed to ensure that every new hire has an opportunity to become steeped in what the company does and how it operates.

The result is called New Employee Orientation (NEO). Today, NEO is a weeklong program held seven times a year at company headquarters in either Evanston, IL, or in one of two locations in India (Pune and New Delhi). The objective of NEO is simple, according to Jeff Griese, chief human resources officer at ZS: "To make our culture come to life."

To do so, NEO includes these elements:

- A focus on three critical aspects of the company: "Who We Are" (heritage, history, and culture), "What We Do" (services, clients, and markets), and "How We Do It" (practices and processes).

- Active participation from senior leaders, including company founders Andy Zoltners and Prabha Sinha and managing director Jaideep Bajaj. "Having the opportunity to meet senior leaders, and listen to the stories they have to share and how they speak about the firm means a lot to new employees," says Griese.

- A chance to get to know other new employees, as well as principals and associates from throughout the firm. Each NEO includes evening social events attended by employees from the local office.

- An opportunity to participate in a simulated client engagement. NEO includes an add-on module called "Jump Start" that gives new employees entering ZS at a more experienced level a chance to solve a typical client challenge in a short amount of time. Since ZS principals play the role of clients, there's a fair amount of pressure, but Jump Start is also a bonding experience.

- A strong sense of what *not* to include in NEO. Since the program's focus is on the company, ZS handles all other information in other ways. For example, new hires are invited to a web session before they start at the company to answer questions ranging from "What time should I arrive at work?" to "What should I wear?" And a separate web meeting is scheduled with new employees to review benefits, payroll, and other HR issues.

# Positive Feedback for NEO

What do new employees think of the ZS orientation program? Feedback is overwhelmingly positive. Here's a sampling:

- "It was inspiring to have the opportunity to hear one of the cofounders speak. The presentation helped put the company's background and goals as well as my role at ZS into perspective. I'm glad Andy and Prabha are presenters in the first days of NEO. It's important to have their presence at this event as a first impression."

- "This was very thought-provoking and did more to give me a positive perception of ZS culture than anything else I've seen thus far."

- "The exercises were helpful in practicing—the session was very interactive, kept our attention, and helped me understand how ZS expects the project process to occur."

- "The mock project was helpful because we actually got to work with our tools. I felt much more comfortable going into my first day of work."

- "The session about the four main project areas and the associate's role helped answer a lot of questions."

- "Very good session; got me excited about ZS."

NEO is obviously a big investment, but it's proven its value, says Griese. "It's important to get employees up to speed as quickly as possible and to make sure they're heading in the right direction," he explains. "NEO is obviously just the beginning of the journey—our managers spend a lot of their time nurturing their people—but we've found that a great start leads to faster and higher impact with our clients."

# Checklist for Giving New Employees What They Need to Be Successful

✓ Think about what new employees need to know about your company, its products or services, its history, and other essential topics.

✓ Ask key stakeholders—including senior leaders, managers, and current employees—what would make a new hire's orientation experience meaningful.

✓ Make sure managers understand their role in orientation.

✓ Give managers a checklist or "playbook" for what they need to do, with background material and resources to draw on.

✓ Have a clear idea of what your orientation program needs to focus on—and what you'll share with new employees through other channels.

✓ Think outside the PowerPoint, creating a format for an orientation program that actively involves employees.

# 12

## Policies

*In this chapter, you learn how to*

- *Describe policies in conversational language that's easy to understand*
- *Organize an employee handbook to describe all your company policies*
- *Bring policies to life*
- *Help employees navigate those times when a number of benefits and policies intersect*

When it comes to aspects of your job that make you jump out of bed in the morning, we bet that "communicating policies" doesn't make the list. Yet you're well aware of how important it is for employees to understand and follow HR policies such as paid time off and dress code. The challenge is that communicating about policies is always a balancing act. On one hand, policies have to be simple enough to be easily understood and acted on. On the other hand, policies have to be precise enough and complete enough (hello, Legal department!) to protect the company. It's no wonder that you sometimes want to shut off your alarm and hide under the covers! But never fear. We're here to help you tackle the policies challenge.

# Here's What I Expect from You and What You Can Expect from Me

Human Resources policies are "the formal rules and guidelines that businesses put in place to hire, train, assess, and reward the members of their workforce" according to USLegal, a company that provides legal templates and forms. We think of policies as an agreement: They give employees information about what the company expects of them and what they can expect from the company.

As a result, "when organized and disseminated in an easily used form...policies can preempt many misunderstandings between employees and employers about their rights and obligations in the business place." Again, that's from USLegal, and we couldn't have said it better ourselves.

Speaking of legal matters, you'll want to get advice from experts in employment law when you communicate many topics to employees, including your policies. The language of the law is quite different from the conversational, easy-to-understand language that helps create effective HR communications, but it is possible to write about company policies and benefits in an interesting and readable way, and still meet legal requirements.

# Policies: The Short Form

Remember the 1984 movie *Gremlins*? While on a business trip to New York City, a dad stops in Chinatown to buy his young son a furry little pet called a mogwai. The shop owner gives three rules for taking care of the pet: Don't get him wet. Keep him away from bright light. And never feed him after midnight. When water is accidentally spilled on the mogwai, it causes him to multiply, producing a number of little brothers. And when the creatures find food after midnight, they turn into scaly monsters called gremlins, and all heck breaks loose.

Policies are a lot like that. You start with one. It's kind of cute. It's easy to take care of. Then you spill coffee on it and suddenly you have a pile of policies. They keep multiplying. And one night when you're working late, you leave a bag of Doritos on your desk—and you can imagine the rest.

For example, when we helped a company create a guide for people managers, we got to spend a lot of time with the company's policies—all 66 of them. Here's a partial list:

- Holidays
- Jury duty
- Military leave
- Vacation
- Job requisitions
- Relocation
- Sending flowers to employees
- Sexual harassment
- Conflict of interest
- Bulletin boards
- Substance abuse

How can you articulate each policy so that it makes sense? How can you organize all these policies so that employees can find them when they need them? We suggest that you start by creating an employee handbook.

# Here's Your Friendly Handbook. Don't Be Frightened. It Won't Bite.

Here's our premise: Policies form an important part of the employment equation, so let's make it easy (and enjoyable, even) for employees to learn more about them.

A handbook can do that for you. It helps new employees understand the rules of the road. It also serves as a reference for longer-term employees—a place to double-check how much time off they get or what to wear when visiting corporate headquarters. In short, a handbook provides information that helps employees succeed (so that the company does, too).

The handbook doesn't need to be a huge document, or an expensive one. It doesn't even have to be a printed document—it can be posted on your intranet or sent via e-mail.

But here's the most important point about creating a handbook: It can't be scary. Yes, a handbook must protect a company from legal problems, but it can't seem like it's written by lawyers. It needs to draw employees in and make them feel comfortable, not send them screaming into the night.

## Our Happy Handbook

A decade or so ago, Alison's company (Davis & Company) was growing, and it needed to collect and communicate its policies in a more organized way. So we decided to create a handbook. We were well aware of the shoemaker's children syndrome (the ones with no shoes): What we created for ourselves absolutely had to practice what we preached.

So, we developed our first handbook. Since then, we've refined it a number of times. And today, we're proud of our employee handbook: We think it exemplifies what a small-company handbook should be.

Let's show you how it works. It's organized into three sections:

- About this handbook
- Our work together
- Company benefits

In "About this handbook," you'll find a photo of a welcome mat and these sentences:

> Welcome to the Davis & Company employee handbook. This book contains policies, benefits, and general information you may need to know as a Davis & Company employee.

> Since our inception, Davis & Company has striven to provide a fun, friendly atmosphere filled with smart people working hard to do great work for our clients.

This employee handbook is designed to provide you with a top-level overview of policies and benefits in an easy-to-read, visual format. The information is kept short on purpose, since we're not a culture with a lot of rules and regulations.

Now for the legal wording: This handbook is to be used as a guide. It is not a contract, expressed or implied, and can be revised at any time.

In just a few sentences, the handbook spells out what it's like to work here and what the new employee can expect to find in the guide. Throughout the handbook, we maintain the same friendly tone while explaining as clearly as possible the policies employees need to know about. Here are some examples:

**Dress code**

Dress appropriately when representing the company. When visiting a client location, please dress appropriately for the client's culture. When a client is visiting the office, dress "business casual."

**Sickness, personal emergencies, or late arrivals**

In case of an unexpected illness, emergency, or late arrival, please send an e-mail to the staff or call the office (or have someone call on your behalf) prior to—or at the start of—the workday. The person who takes your call will put the information on the electronic calendar and share it with the staff via e-mail. If you miss work for two hours or more, enter it on your timesheet as paid time off.

**Paid time off**

Davis & Company's system classifies all types of time off— vacations, holidays, sick time, personal time, and any other nonbusiness time away from the office during normal work hours—as paid time off. All of these—tracked in two-hour increments—are deducted from your bank of accrued paid time. Any paid time off that is less than two hours should be made up within that week.

[This is the introduction; it continues from here.]

# Do Your Homework Before Producing Your Handbook

If you're beginning a project to create an employee handbook, here are some great ways to start.

First, do your homework. Conduct research with the following:

- **Employees and managers.** Find out what each isn't hearing from the other. Ask, "What do you wish you knew on Day One but didn't?"

- **Plan providers, call centers, and so on.** What do your employees not know, need to know, need to do better for themselves? What mistakes are employees making?

- **Company programs and program and plan managers.** Find out what is working well, what is not, what you wish every employee knew about your program.

- **Employee surveys or questionnaires.** What trends do you see in terms of misunderstood programs or procedures?

- **Senior managers.** What do they want every employee to know, do, and feel? What is driving them crazy right now?

This is a great start to finding out what is working, and what's not, in your organization. What's really great about this process is that *you* might be the person to change what's not working at your company into what *is* working, simply by doing your job and communicating well.

## Establish Your Objectives

Based on what you learned in your research, set up three overall objectives for your employee handbook, and determine how you will measure the success of each. For example:

| If your objective is to: | You might measure success by: |
| --- | --- |
| Help employees take advantage of company programs and services | Tracking employee usage of various programs or measuring the overall increase in usage |
| Reduce time not working (loss of productivity) caused by mistakes employees make in presenting medical claims | Measure percentages of mistakes in claims, and set a goal of reducing mistakes by X% (which increases productivity) |

## Gather Content

Now it's time to gather content. An employee handbook typically covers topics that Human Resources manages: policies, benefits, and programs to help the business attract and keep talented performers.

Ideally, your employee handbook also includes information from staff areas throughout the company: Information Technology, Facilities, Legal, Human Resources, Marketing, Public Affairs, Investor or Shareholder Relations, Training, Community Relations. All these functional areas have information to contribute to help employees know what to do in a variety of situations and how to use the services or resources that each area offers.

Employees don't think about company programs and services coming from a variety of internal functions; it's all "from the company" to them. It's silly for each staff function to produce its own version of a handbook, because that weighs heavily on the arms of employees. That's why it's good to have descriptions of all the services and programs offered by all the staff functions in one resource in print and online.

## Organize Your Handbook in a Way That Makes Sense for Your Company and Your Employees

After you've gathered all the background material, you need to organize it. You can use a number of different criteria to do so:

- Timeline of the employment relationship (from joining the company through leaving)
- Alphabetical order by policy
- Order of importance or order of value to your employees (most to least)
- Order of cost (most expensive to least)
- Life events (see more in the sidebar "The Truth About Killing Trees," in Chapter 3, "Plan and Manage Communication")

Once you have identified all your content and have organized it in some fashion, look for even bigger labels to put on the content so it will appeal to your readers. Here is an example of what we mean.

## Financial Services Firm

Here is how Jane organized the contents of an employee handbook for a small financial services firm that wanted to keep its low turnover rate. This was a simple 12-page brochure the company could use in recruiting and orientation and as a reference for its current staff. Copy from the handbook's inside front cover said, "To continue our success, we seek to attract, motivate, and encourage long-term employment of talented, service-oriented people."

The handbook was organized by importance, starting with pay, and then covering topics in order of sequence, ending with retirement. Here is an overview of the content:

**Creating your wealth**

- Compensation philosophy
- Your base salary
- Annual incentive plan
- 401(k) savings plan
- Employee stock purchase plan
- Sales incentive awards
- Discounts on company products and services

**Maintaining your good health**

- Medical and dental plans
- Healthcare, child care, elder care reimbursement accounts

**Protecting your future**

- Life insurance
- Dependent life insurance
- Short- and long-term disability
- Business travel accident insurance

**Building your skills**

- Company training programs
- Tuition reimbursement program
- Scholarships for children of employees

**Balancing your work and personal life**

- Holidays, vacation, and personal days
- Family and medical leave
- Wedding gift program
- Employee assistance program
- Dependent care
- Matching gifts for education

**Providing for your retirement**

- Your retirement program

**Investing in you**

(A chart overview of company benefits, when you're eligible, and who pays.)

Jane organized the contents based on what the company offered and what employees valued, and then created a series of parallel subheadings, each starting with a gerund. Simply reading the table of contents tells you a lot about the culture of a company and the employment proposition.

### *Other Ways to Organize*

In another employee handbook we created, we organized information into the following section headings, starting with the basics and then following a more-or-less sequential organization:

- Our work environment
- Getting started
- On the job
- Compensation
- Employee benefits, programs, and services
- Time off
- Problem solving
- Leaving
- Resources

And for still another handbook, here's how we organized the content:

- How we work
- On the job
- Money matters
- Time off
- Benefits for you
- Solving problems
- Leaving the company

# Desperately Seeking Information

Whichever structure you use to organize your handbook, keep this in mind: Employees will need help finding just the information they want. Even if you conducted research with managers and employees and put your handbook together accordingly, some employees will look for the topic of "life insurance" in the "pay" section instead of "benefits." Or perhaps they don't consider "sick days" time off, so they'd never think to look for that topic in that section.

You need to do three things to make it easier for employees to find what they need:

- **Create a detailed list of contents at the front of the handbook (or on the homepage, if it's online).** Don't just list "benefits"; list specifics such as "vision care" or "tuition reimbursement" with a page number (if your handbook is in print) or link.

- **If your handbook is in print, include an index.** Book publishers tell us that roughly 50% of all people go to the table of contents to find a topic, and 50% head for the index. That's why it's important to have both in your handbook: You make it easy for 100% of your audience to find what they're looking for.

- **If your handbook is online, make sure the search function works well.** Work with your Information Technology department or vendor to ensure that content is tagged properly. That way, employees can, for example, type "corporate credit card" in the search box and go right to the page they need.

# Keep the Language Conversational— Please, No Legalese

As you write your handbook, read it aloud to hear if it sounds like one employee talking with another. As we said previously, you do not want the handbook to sound like a lawyer writing to employees (even if you work in a law firm).

Although it's true that more employees today sue their current or former employers, the employees who sue represent an extremely small percentage of your total employee handbook readership. You're preparing the handbook for the majority of employees—those wonderful folks who will never sue you. Nothing you say in the employee handbook will ever *prevent* someone from suing your company. What you say should *encourage* most employees to do a good job.

Including quotes from real employees (along with their photos) is a great way to share the unwritten secrets of success in your environment. For example, in one of the employee handbooks we produced, an employee was quoted as follows: "We never have *problems* here; we only have *opportunities*." (Emphasis is as the employee stated.) When you include quotes from employees, giving advice about how to succeed in the organization, you're not only sharing great advice; you're also recognizing those employees featured as being successful.

## About ID Cards

One of the handbooks Jane created had a section on ID cards. Here are the first two paragraphs:

> You received an identification (ID) card during your processing appointment when you first joined us. It includes your name, signature, personnel number, and a probably not-very-flattering photo.

> You should always carry your ID card when you come to work, because you'll need it to enter most of our facilities and to prove your eligibility for some employee services.

Note the phrase "a probably not-very-flattering photo." It indicates that a real human being wrote the handbook. It's a small way for a "voice" to be heard—the voice of one employee talking to another. That's the tone of voice you should strive for: an employee sharing good advice with a colleague.

# Encourage Employees to Use the Handbook as a Resource

The ideal place to distribute the employee handbook is during the orientation process. If you can pull it off, one of the best ways to make employees familiar with the handbook's contents is to hold a competition during an orientation program. You would ask teams of employees to find answers to some of the questions in the handbook. The first team with all the right answers wins.

Education professionals will tell you that if you give a person a resource, and the person *actually uses* that resource within the first hour of receiving it, the chances increase exponentially that the person will use that resource again.

# Put a Title on Your Work

"Working Together" works well as a title for an employee handbook. It indicates that we're all in this together, and having some common understandings about how we'll work together makes sense.

Here are some additional thoughts about good titles for employee handbooks:

- "How to Succeed at [Your Company Name]"
- "73 Reasons Why [Your Company Name] Is a Great Place to Work"
- "How You Bring Good Things to Light at GE" (tie in with advertising slogans)
- "The Benefits of a Career with [Your Company Name]"

# Measure Results

Include a one-page survey in the employee handbook or on the web page that offers some incentive to employees to complete it and turn it in. This could be a free lunch at a nearby restaurant or the company cafeteria. Also track before-and-after data regarding usage of company programs. Pick a few key goals you set up as a result of your research, and then check back with program managers, call centers, and so on to see what improvements have occurred since you produced the employee handbook.

Hold focus group sessions about six months after distributing the employee handbook. Determine what questions employees still have, what sections confuse them, and what information they want included that isn't there.

Use what you learn to improve the intranet version of your handbook immediately, and update the print version at least every two years.

# Bring Policies to Life

Of course, even the best-written policy may need support to encourage employees to learn about it and take action on it. For example, a financial services company created a flexible work arrangements policy to allow employees to work on a different schedule or from home. But the company learned that many employees didn't know about the policy, and many managers were skeptical. They believed that the terms "flexibility" and "work" were mutually exclusive.

We helped the company communicate with both employees and managers about two aspects of the policy: the benefits of working flexibly, and how employees (and managers) start and successfully manage such an arrangement.

Sharing the policy itself was certainly the beginning of our communication efforts. But even more important was bringing the policy to life by doing the following:

- Using research to demonstrate the value of flexible work arrangements to show how they can improve productivity and job satisfaction
- Giving examples of different aspects of flexible work arrangements, such as flextime (starting and ending times), flexplace (telecommuting), compressed workweek (full-time work completed in fewer than five days), and job sharing (two employees share the responsibilities of one full-time job)
- Providing all the paperwork needed to set up an arrangement, with clear instructions on how to fill it out
- Helping managers and employees deal with potential pitfalls by communicating scenarios and how to resolve them
- Giving managers and employees a chance to get their questions answered by including FAQs in the print and written communication and by holding learning sessions they can attend in person or via web meeting

# Communicate Life Events When Policies, Programs, and Benefits Intersect

If you think about the various life events that an employee can experience while working at your company, you may find you need to take extra steps in communicating what happens when various programs, policies, and benefits intersect.

Life events can include getting married, having a baby, moving into a new home, being sick or injured, caring for an older or younger relative, and more. Sometimes, a simple chart can illustrate what happens when.

For more-complex subjects, we like to take a visual approach. For example, having a baby is a life event where provisions from your medical plan combine with policies about parental leave, vacation, and other time-off policies. Having a baby might even require changes in other benefit plans. We found we needed more space than a simple chart to show a timeline with color coding to show which plans or policies kicked in at which point. Our resulting communication was a horizontal placemat-sized document that quickly showed a parent-to-be when he or she was eligible for which time-off provision and how this could be extended with vacation time. It also noted places where the parent needed to take action (to include the new baby in health coverage, for example) as well as information and resources the parent could receive.

# Checklist for Making the Most of All That Your Company Offers

To make sure your employees take advantage of everything your company offers, you'll want to do the following:

- ✓ Articulate your policies in a clear, simple way, using nonlegal language.
- ✓ Create a handbook that's geared toward helping employees find policy information quickly and easily.
- ✓ Use employee quotes and examples to make policies more vivid.
- ✓ Bring policies such as flexible work arrangements to life.
- ✓ Create clear visuals that show how your programs, policies, and benefits intersect during important life events such as getting married and having a baby.

# 13

## Benefits

*In this chapter, you learn how to*

- *Create benefits communication simpler, faster, and easier*
- *Help employees understand their benefits so they can make smart choices and use benefits wisely*
- *Give employees good reasons to appreciate the benefits your company offers*

## "My Head Hurts"

It comes around every year: benefits enrollment season. And every year you work hard to communicate benefits so that employees will understand your plan (or choice of plans) and take appropriate action.

But every year the task gets more difficult. Healthcare costs keep rising. Plan rules get more complicated. You make changes to keep costs contained, and employees view those changes as "takeaways." And just when you think you've got it all under control, a big curveball (can you say "healthcare reform"?) comes along.

It's no wonder that every year you end up with a headache that requires a jumbo bottle of extra-strength pain reliever. (Which reminds you that you need to let employees know that over-the-counter medicines can no longer be reimbursed on their flexible spending account.)

We can't take away your headache, but we *can* take the pain out of communicating benefits—both during the enrollment period and throughout the year. In this chapter, we show you how.

Along the way, we give examples from a company Alison's firm has worked with over the past several years to communicate benefits to its employees. For a variety of reasons, we can't share the company's real name, so we call it Walnut, Inc. Headquartered in the New York City area, Walnut has operations throughout North America with 25,000 employees in various functions, including research, manufacturing, sales, and distribution.

# Is Eight Your Lucky Number?

It's ours when it comes to benefits communication. We've found that following these eight steps make communicating benefits more effective:

1. Set objectives for what your company wants to achieve.
2. Understand employees' needs and preferences.
3. Develop a planned approach.
4. Communicate simply, clearly, and candidly.
5. Manage time wisely.
6. Use tools for what they do best.
7. Focus on what employees need to do.
8. Measure progress and success.

### *Again, Begin with Objectives*

As we said earlier, we believe that most communication projects should start with the end in mind, so you should set objectives for what you want to accomplish. (See Chapter 3, "Plan and Manage

Communication," for a lot of advice about how to do so.) This is especially true when you're communicating benefits. Why? Because you often need employees to take actions that determine whether your benefits are successful. The idea, of course, is to make sure you design communications to support employees taking those actions.

For example, each year the benefits team at Walnut, Inc. sets objectives for desired employee behavior. Here is a sample:

- Increase participation in the long-term disability program.
- Reduce the number of calls to the HR service center (the vendor company that handles enrollment and other calls).
- Influence employees to sign up for benefits throughout the enrollment period. (The idea is to encourage them not to wait until the last two or three days to do so.)
- Encourage a percentage of employees to switch from the "preferred" PPO plan (more choices, higher premiums) to the "select" plan (fewer choices, lower premiums).

### Understand What Employees Know and What They Need

Once you're clear about what your company wants to accomplish, it's time to turn your focus to employee needs and preferences. As we describe in Chapter 1, "Know Your Employees," qualitative research—such as focus groups—helps you find out the following:

- How well employees understand their current benefits. Don't assume that just because you've communicated the vision plan for the past five years that employees know about the importance of those benefits and how they work. You must dive deeper to get an accurate assessment.
- Perceptions about the value of benefits. Do employees appreciate what they have, or do they undervalue the program?
- What employees need to know—and how they want to receive communication.

## What You Can Learn by Asking

One of the first things that Walnut's new director of compensation and benefits did when he started his job was to talk informally with a few colleagues to find out what they thought of the company's current benefits. Their answer—that the company's benefits were not as good as those offered by competitors—surprised the director, because his benchmarking research had found that Walnut's benefits were comparable to or even better than other similar companies. He wondered: Did all employees share this misconception?

To find out, the director asked us to survey a sample of employees as well as conduct several focus groups. Research results confirmed that employees thought their benefits were worse than those offered at other companies and that Walnut was reducing benefits. The root cause of this belief? Employees had a low understanding of both their healthcare plans and their total benefits package.

The research also shed light on employees' communication preferences:

- Employees didn't want surprises. They'd rather that change occur gradually than be caught off guard by something drastic.

- When changes were made, employees wanted clear, candid communication.

- Employees needed benefits information in one place and preferred to look at enrollment information at home (at the kitchen table).

- The ideal way to present health plan choices? Employees requested a side-by-side, "apples to apples" comparison.

- Employees wanted communication to be easy to read and navigate.

## Develop a Planned Approach

If you've followed steps 1 (set objectives) and 2 (find out what employees know and what they need), you have a strong basis for developing your approach to benefits communication.

Let's use the Walnut example to explain what we mean. You'll recall that the HR team had specific actions it wanted employees to take. And employees clearly expressed what they needed. In their own words, employees said:

- "Tell me what's changing and what to do."
- "Don't sugarcoat it—give me the facts."
- "Comparisons and examples would be helpful."
- "Make it easy for me to make the right decision."

Putting these together helped Walnut's benefits director decide how to communicate to meet both HR's objectives and employees' needs. Here's an excerpt from the planning tool we used to choose the right communication approach:

| Company Objective | Employee Need | Communication Approach |
|---|---|---|
| Employees will have a better understanding and greater appreciation of benefits | Benefits information in one place, with enrollment materials mailed to them at home | A print handbook that highlights health plan information and describes other benefits, including life insurance and tuition assistance |
| Employees will make smart choices about which health plan to enroll in and will use the plan wisely | To compare health plan choices "apples to apples" | Overview of plans in the handbook, plus an at-a-glance "spreadsheet" insert |
| Employees will place fewer calls to the HR Service Center | Materials that are easy to read and navigate | Use of sections, color, table of contents, index, and other navigation tools, both in print and online

Tone is clear, friendly, service-oriented |

## Communicate Simply, Clearly, and Candidly

We're so passionate about being simple, clear, and candid that we could write a book about the topic—oh, right, we're doing that here. But our advice especially applies to benefits. Because your company offers so many different benefits, and because many of them are so complex, it's even more important that you simplify, simplify, simplify how you communicate. Here are a few tips about how to do so (some are reminders from previous chapters):

- **Use the inverted pyramid to organize information.** This classic structure puts the most relevant information first and saves the details for lower down in the message. And it works for any kind of communication, from e-mail to enrollment packages to benefits meetings.

- **Focus on what employees need to do.** In these information-overloaded times, employees want you to cut to the chase and tell them what action is required. So be clear, with content such as "Five decisions you need to make" and "A three-step process for choosing your benefits."

- **Be visual.** Instead of long narrative copy, break content into easily scannable segments. For example, create a table that captures key changes to next year's benefits. Or add a sidebar with a checklist of decision items. And whenever possible, use icons, photos, or sketches to illustrate your points.

- **Avoid the urge to sugarcoat.** Communicating benefits is often a "bad news, bad news" proposition. Sometimes costs increase; other times benefits are eliminated. To maintain credibility, it's important to communicate honestly. Tell employees why a change was made, how costs were managed, and how they can choose and spend wisely.

- **Don't be shy about celebrating good things.** Use communication to remind employees about benefits that are designed to make their lives better, such as flexible spending account debit cards, preventive care, discount gym memberships, and free financial advice.

- **Be service-oriented.** Include tips, advice, and Q&As that will help employees be smarter consumers and live healthier. Here are some examples of service-oriented topics you can integrate into your communications:
  - How to determine if you're saving enough for retirement
  - Low-impact ways to get more exercise
  - How I saved $300 on my prescriptions
  - Five often overlooked discounts offered by the company medical plan
- **Tell the "why" behind benefits changes.** While you want to focus on what's new and what employees need to do, sometimes it's also important to remind employees why your company provides these benefits and the process you go through before making any changes. Chances are, senior leaders gave benefits changes a lot of thought, looked through the data, and made strategic decisions based on cost-benefit analysis. Walk employees through that process and present this information as a sidebar in your communication.

### Give Benefits Communication a Much-Needed Voice

Here's one more piece of advice under the category "simple, clear, and candid": Don't lose the human side of the equation. It's easy to get so wrapped up in getting the facts right that you forget that communication should feel personal. After all, benefits are a topic that employees take personally. Our colleague Kimberly Gavagan recently wrote a blog for the Davis & Company website that captures this idea so well that we'd like to share it with you:

> A friend of mine recently received an envelope in the mail from the life insurance provider for her company. When my friend opened it, she found generic materials sent directly from the vendor—with not even a cover letter from her own company explaining what was inside.
>
> Her company is family-owned. Leaders make an effort to get to know employees and make them feel valued.

This generic, no-personality package was the opposite of what Sasha is used to. It contained a standard brochure and a bland form asking her to select one of two options for her life insurance coverage. There was no indication that this was part of her company's benefits program.

Sasha was baffled. And honestly, so am I.

This strikes me as a missed opportunity. Every time you send something to your employees about benefits, you are sending two messages. The first, of course, is the information itself.

The second is silent, yet speaks volumes: It's about creating a sense of connection between company and employee. In this case, the connection was lacking and the tone was saying, "We don't care."

Benefits are an emotional issue for employees. They see benefits as a way to take care of themselves and their families, provide financial security in the event of an illness or injury, and help them happily retire.

This is not the time for generic communication.

If you must use the materials your vendor supplies, at least provide employees with a little context: a cover note explaining what's coming, why it's important, and what employees should do.

Even better, benefits communication should align with your company's brand. Model it after your company's ads. Write simply, avoid jargon, and be straightforward.

The best path, of course, is to make benefits communication personal. Employees should feel like it's coming from a human being—one who works at their company and understands them—and not a warehouse.

By doing so, you not only build understanding about benefits, but also create goodwill as well.

## How Walnut Keeps It Simple

Benefits communication at Walnut exemplifies simplicity, clarity, and candor. Here are three examples:

1. **A poster (displayed outside cafeterias and on bulletin boards)**

   It's time for open enrollment.

   Review your benefits for next year.

   Act now to take advantage of new, lower rates for Voluntary Long-Term Disability and Life Insurance.

   Enroll by November 28.

2. **Introduction to a resource book (available online and printed for new employees) that contains information on all Walnut benefits**

   Your life is complicated. There's so much to do, so much to experience, with a change around every corner. You get married. Get a promotion. Buy a house. Send your first child off to college. Start thinking about retirement.

   Walnut benefits are designed to provide a comprehensive program to help meet your healthcare, insurance, work/life, and retirement needs. But like everything else in life, making the best use of your benefits takes effort. By taking an active role in learning what choices are available, selecting the benefits that fit your needs, and using your benefits wisely, you will get the most out of these valuable assets.

   This resource book is designed to help you get started. It provides an overview of all your benefits, with helpful hints on each. Use this information to begin the process of becoming informed about benefits, taking advantage of websites and other resources to explore specific benefits in more detail.

3. **A chart explaining changes to the PPO plans**

   Basic and Select PPO Plans will become Enhanced PPO.

   Walnut will offer the Enhanced PPO Plan, which will replace the Basic and Select PPO Plans, starting January 1 next year.

*continued*

The Enhanced PPO will combine features of both PPOs, as shown in the following chart:

| | Current PPO Plans | | New PPO Plan |
|---|---|---|---|
| What's Changing | This Year's Basic | This Year's Select | Next Year's Enhanced |
| Office visit copayment | $20 nonspecialist $40 specialist | $20 nonspecialist $40 specialist | $25 nonspecialist $40 specialist |
| Outpatient coverage | 85% coinsurance with an out-of-pocket maximum of $2,400 individual/$4,800 family | 100% coinsurance | 90% coinsurance with an out-of-pocket maximum of $1,250 individual/$2,500 family |
| Inpatient coverage | 85% coinsurance | $250/day copay with an 8-day copay maximum of $2,000 per year | $500/day copay with a 2-day copay maximum of $1,000 per year |

## Manage Time Wisely

When it comes to benefits communication, the Rolling Stones got it wrong: Time is definitely not on your side. In fact, timing is one of the trickiest aspects of communicating benefits, as shown here:

| | |
|---|---|
| Provide information too early, and employees are likely to ignore it. | "I'll get to that later." |
| Send messages too often, and employees will think there will be more, so they can wait to act. | "I'll catch the next one." |
| Send too much information, such as daily e-mails for a month. | "This is really annoying. I'll just keep pressing the delete key." |
| Communicate just in time, and employees will respond in a timely manner. | "I'll do this right now." |
| Give information too late, and employees will feel blind-sided. | "Wait! Wait! I need more time!" |

We don't have a hard-and-fast rule for managing time wisely. Instead, in each situation, we work at achieving the right balance. We seek to give employees enough time to understand an upcoming change so that they can get used to it. And we give employees a heads-up when something is coming. ("Next month is when enroll-ment starts.") But we also want to be as "just in time" as possible so that employees have the information right before they need to take action. Finally, we're big fans of "friendly reminders"—short mes-sages that don't overwhelm or annoy, but give employees a gentle push to get going.

The best way to manage timing, we find, is to create a timeline as part of your communication plan (see Chapter 3). That way, you can map out how employees will learn about benefits and ensure that the timing creates understanding and encourages people to take action. Figure 13-1 shows what we mean.

| Element | Audience | Activity | Dates |
|---|---|---|---|
| Employee Benefits Update–September | U.S. (non-PR), non-union, employees | Employees receive newsletter–printed version | 9/15 |
| Leader Briefings | Senior HR/senior management | Hold senior leader meetings | 10/17 |
| HR Portal | U.S. union and non-union | Site changes launched | Week of 11/5 |
| Health Fairs | Employees at key locations | Health fair in Madison | 11/5-11/28 |
| Posters and Screens | U.S. union and non-union employees | OE posters in locations | 11/15-11/26 |
| Reminder E-mails | U.S. (non-PR) employees | Distribute e-mail #2 | Week of 10/29 |
| Open Enrollment Package | U.S. (non-PR), non-union employees | Employees receive kits | Week of 10/22 |
| Employee Benefits Update–October | U.S. (non-PR), non-union employees | Employees receive newsletter with OE Package | 10/15 |

**Figure 13-1  Communication timeline**

*More Examples: "Here's a Preview" and "Don't Forget"*

Our friends at Walnut think a lot about timing. One technique that's worked well is to provide a heads-up about upcoming benefit changes about a month before open enrollment begins:

### Preview of Benefit Changes for Next Year

Many employees have said it is helpful to learn about changes in advance of Open Enrollment. While you'll find details of next year's benefit changes in your Open Enrollment packet in early October, here's a preview of what's changing.

For next year, Walnut has made changes that keep projected healthcare cost increases under control and also has added plan features that can save you money and time. This includes important changes to the medical plans, Health Care Spending Account, and voluntary life insurance. Read on to learn more.

Once enrollment begins, Walnut sends e-mail, displays posters, and mails postcards designed to provide gentle reminders to employees. For example, here's a personalized e-mail sent only to employees who have not yet enrolled:

### Don't wait until the last day to enroll!

Our records show that you have not yet made your benefit elections for next year. If you are not currently enrolled in Long-Term Disability coverage, don't miss out on this one-time opportunity to join the plan without submitting evidence of good health.

Also, you must enroll in the Health Care and/or Dependent Care Flexible Spending Accounts if you want to participate in these accounts next year.

The deadline for enrolling in all these plans is November 29.

Enroll online by visiting www.mybenefits.com.

Enroll by phone by calling 800-XXX-XXXX.

If this is your first time enrolling online, at the Login screen, enter your social security number in the "user name" field and the last four digits of your employee ID number in the "PIN" field.

Questions? Call the HR Service Center at 800-XXX-XXXX.

The result of making an investment in timing? Walnut has been able to achieve one of its main objectives: persuade employees to act throughout enrollment, and not wait until the last minute to sign up. (This saves the company money by not incurring extra vendor charges and also reduces errors.) For instance, by giving employees information in advance during one year's open enrollment, Walnut persuaded them to sign up early:

*This Year's Daily Enrollment Was More Balanced Than Last Year's*

| Time Period | Last Year Enrollees | This Year Enrollees | Change |
| --- | --- | --- | --- |
| First 3 days | 1,768 | 3,117 | +76% |
| Last 3 days | 8,982 | 7,344 | –18% |

## Use Tools for What They Do Best

We talk a lot about tools in Chapter 7, "Use the Right Tool for the Job," so we'll be brief here. In fact, we can boil down our advice to one sentence: When it comes to benefits communication, don't use e-mail for everything.

E-mail is great for timely reminders. And for quick checklists. And to provide handy links to information available on a website.

But e-mail is not as effective as other communication channels for conveying complex information. For instance, we love web tools that help employees enter personalized data and calculate the best choices for them. And we love posters and postcards for providing important information at a glance.

However, we must confess that our favorite tool for communicating benefits is still, after all these years, a print publication. Whether it's a brief flyer (such as a "Slim Jim" that fits into a #10 standard envelope), a four-page newsletter, or a full brochure, we find that print fits the bill for the following:

- Compiling all the facts that employees need to understand benefits and make decisions
- Including charts, tables, and other ways to compare information
- Bringing benefits to life through examples
- Allowing employees to share information with significant others

## Walnut Says, "Print It"

Like many companies, about 10 years ago Walnut discontinued its open enrollment mailing and went to a strictly online format. But when we asked employees what they thought about the change, here's what they said:

- Employees weren't getting the full story from the website, just bits and pieces. That contributed to their lack of understanding about benefits.

- Since employees preferred print, they were creating their own packages by printing web pages. But that wasn't as effective as a well-designed print piece.

- Employees perceived the move to online-only information as another takeaway. "Bring back our printed information!" was a typical comment.

As a result, Walnut reinstated its enrollment package—the first year as a full brochure with information about all company benefits, and in subsequent years as a newsletter (which was also available online). Walnut also started using print when communicating about specific benefits, such as disability and tuition reimbursement. Figure 13-2 shows a flyer distributed in information racks near cafeterias, break rooms, and facility entrances.

## Are you enrolled in the Long-Term Disability Plan?

**If not, don't miss out on this one-time opportunity to enroll!**

**You can't afford not to.**

**How would you take care of your family if you had no income?**

Protect your income if an illness or accident keeps you out of work.

Did you know?

• People in their 30s are three times more likely to suffer a disability than die.
  - National Association of Insurance Commissioners

• Almost three in 10 workers entering the workforce today will become disabled before retiring.
  -Council for Disability Awareness

• Unexpected disabilities caused at least 17% of personal bankruptcies in 2001.
  -Council for Disability Awareness

**Figure 13-2 Benefits flyer**

### Emphasize Action

One thing we like about benefits communication is that it's action-packed. Seriously. The reason to communicate is not simply to provide information; it's to give employees what they need to do something (and that something usually helps them). So we plan and create our communication keeping desired action steps in mind. We use words and phrases such as these:

- Act now
- What you need to do
- Reminder
- How to
- Don't miss out

## Keeping Track

How can you tell if your action-oriented communication is working? We share some tips on measuring benefits communication in a moment, but we also recommend collecting whatever metrics you can about what employees are doing. Walnut's HR Service Center database allowed HR to keep a close eye on how communication stimulated action. Figure 13-3 shows a sample report.

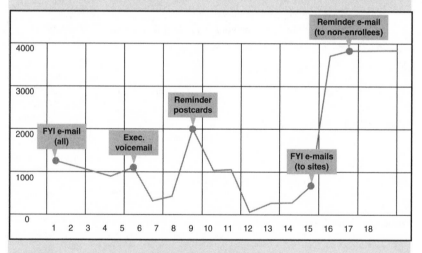

Figure 13-3    Sample communication report

## *Measure Twice; Cut Once*

As we describe in Chapter 9, "Measure Effectiveness," measuring your communication is essential for testing its impact, to demonstrate its value, and also to adjust and improve your communications going forward. You can measure benefits communication in a variety of ways, including spot surveys during and after enrollment, an annual (or biannual) survey, and detailed reporting from your database or vendor systems.

Wondering which questions to ask? Here are a few standard survey questions:

The enrollment package mailed to my home was useful.

Strongly agree     Agree    Disagree    Strongly disagree

I understood the choices available to me.

Strongly agree     Agree    Disagree    Strongly disagree

I felt prepared to make smart decisions about enrollment.

Strongly agree     Agree    Disagree    Strongly disagree

## Walnut Measures Success

How did Walnut know that its benefits communication efforts were successful? Both actions and employee feedback indicated that its communication was meeting employees' needs. For example:

82% of employees agreed that they understood their benefits.

70% felt that the communications were useful.

Here are some employee comments:

"This year's communications on benefits have been extremely valuable. They helped me more thoroughly understand the changes."

"Thank you for providing understandable information in many formats."

"I appreciate the efforts to help me reach a full understanding of the options available."

# Checklist for Helping Employees Understand Their Benefits So That They Know What to Do

✓ Know what you want to accomplish.

✓ Ask employees what they know and need.

✓ Make even the most complicated benefits information simple.

✓ Keep an eye on the calendar to get the timing right.

✓ Don't rely only on e-mail; take out the other tools in your communication toolbox.

✓ Emphasize steps employees need to take, and encourage them to act now.

✓ Measure to demonstrate success and get ready for next time.

# 14

## Compensation

*In this chapter, you learn how to*

- *Communicate clearly about pay*
- *Give employees tools to help them see the value of their compensation*
- *Help prepare managers to talk face-to-face about pay*

## Beware the Black Box

Of all the topics organizations need to communicate, you'd think they'd be most effective at communicating about pay. After all, although you hope that employees love their jobs, they work to earn money—to pay their mortgage, put gas in the car, and buy their children shoes. So employees care deeply about how they're compensated.

But here's the tricky part. Compensation is, appropriately, a delicate subject. For many good reasons, Person A may be paid differently than Person B, even though they're doing the same job. So although you can broadly communicate your philosophy and framework for *how* you pay people, *what* you pay them needs to be discussed privately, between an employee and his or her manager.

Because of the need for confidentiality, companies often undercommunicate about compensation. The result is that employees experience compensation as a "black box"—a device whose workings are incomprehensible and inaccessible. The black box becomes like a frustrating magic trick. Information (such as performance management ratings) goes into the box, a secret process occurs, and what comes out—a salary increase or bonus amount—seems mysterious. This can cause employees to become confused, frustrated, and even unmotivated.

How can you demystify pay so that it engenders positive feelings? Read on.

# Money Does Not Equal Motivation

We would be remiss if we didn't make this point: Money alone is not a motivator. We're a fan of Daniel Pink, whose book *Drive*[1] draws on four decades of scientific research to identify three elements of motivation—autonomy, mastery, and purpose—that surpass money as a motivator. He notes that humans have a deep need "to direct our own lives, to learn and create new things, and to do better by ourselves and our world."

In terms of pay, Pink says most of us just want to know we're being paid equitably both inside and outside our organization. In short, we'd like to think our salary is about what it would be if we left to join a competitor. And we'd like to think that someone with a comparable job inside our company doesn't make a lot more than we do—unless, of course, it's obvious that our colleague merits a lot more money.

We share this information because at the start of any communication challenge, we think it's a good idea to learn a bit more about your topic from outside your company. You'll also want to know how employees in your company feel about pay in order to create communications that will resonate with them.

# The Magic Number Is 5

All the advice we shared with you in Part I of this book applies to communicating about pay, of course, but we especially recommend that you focus on these five strategies:

1. Use simple language
2. Create visuals
3. Help managers talk about pay
4. Personalize, if possible
5. Provide examples to bring numbers to life

### Use Simple Language

Have you heard this advice before? Of course you have—in Chapter 5, "Write Simply and Clearly." But it's worth repeating, because if we see one consistent problem with compensation communication, it's just too complicated.

We know what you're thinking: Communication is complicated because so is compensation these days. It used to be easy when the only component was straight salary. But many companies have added variable pay to the mix, which is tied to company and/or individual performance. Then there are bonuses (also known as short-term incentives). And finally, you may have long-term incentives, which might take the form of stock options or restricted stock.

Have we mentioned everything? Maybe not. Compensation consultants are always coming up with new approaches to paying employees. In any case, we don't disagree that your overall compensation program can get pretty complicated.

But that doesn't mean your communication has to be complicated, too. In fact, the greatest service you can offer employees is to make communication simple, so that employees can understand how even the most gnarly pay plan works.

## Don't Do This

For an example of how not to communicate, we bring you this excerpt from a brochure on compensation created for VPs at a major corporation. (The company name and details have been changed to protect the guilty.)

> Acme pays for performance by directly linking pay levels to company business performance. To ensure that pay levels are aligned with business performance, an analysis is performed each year comparing Acme to relevant peer companies. In this analysis, Acme's performance on key financial metrics is first compared to the performance of a number of direct competitors. Financial metrics may include such items as sales volume, revenue growth, earnings per share, return on investment, and shareholder returns. These financial metrics in aggregate are used to establish a measure of overall company performance. In addition, total compensation, which is comprised of total cash (Base Salary plus Annual and Premium Bonuses) and long-term awards, is compared against the pay levels of more than 13,000 executives in over 500 large companies. This analysis ensures that pay levels reflect emerging marketplace practices and are competitive relative to the market. The completed analysis shows how Acme compares to the peer companies on both overall performance and total compensation by quartile. Acme's targeted level of pay is in the third quartile, which means that, depending on Acme's performance, pay levels will be better than at least half of the companies in the peer group.

Aaaargh! Believe us, it doesn't have to be this way! Here, for example, is the introduction we wrote for a technology company when it launched a new salary structure:

> In this booklet, you'll read about how we manage pay in our company and learn the basics of the new compensation structure. This will supplement the in-person meetings you are having with your manager. The new structure—which features seven salary bands—is being launched this month to all associates.

Why a new compensation structure now? Quite simply, the old one wasn't working very well. A compensation structure should be simple, consistent, and aligned with the business strategy. The old structure, with 32 salary grades, had too many levels, wide disparities within grades, and was applied inconsistently across the businesses. The result was that many of us spent a lot of time talking about pay and experienced frustration trying to figure out how the structure applied to us.

We think the new compensation structure is a big improvement. With seven salary bands, the compensation structure aligns with our business strategy, provides an effective means to pay our people competitively, and recognizes achievements based on individual and company results.

Here's the new structure at a glance:

| Level | Role |
|-------|------|
| 1 | Enterprise leadership |
| 2 | Organizational leadership |
| 3 | Business/system leadership |
| 4 | Business/process driver |
| 5 | Functional specialist |
| 6 | Administrative/technical |
| 7 | Clerical |

Aaaah, that's better, isn't it? Even though pay has changed a lot in the years we've been communicating, the fundamentals—being clear and simple—haven't. For instance, here is the cover copy from a compensation brochure Jane produced some 30 years ago:

Here's something you'll like.

A brochure only for company officers that discusses:

MONEY

Specifically, it covers how you earn it, how you can earn more of it, how you can accumulate it, and how you can protect what you've got.

This straightforward, direct language would encourage potential readers to turn a page or click to get more information as well today as it did in the past. An interesting feature of this brochure was that it summarized features of a special executive compensation program that most of the readers of this brochure were not even eligible for.

Why include this? Although everyone knew about the special executive compensation program, most officers didn't know what it covered. So, instead of talking about it factually, officers would speculate about what must/might be included. Putting a summary in this brochure gave them the facts, so they didn't need to waste time wondering about it. Perhaps it also provided a bit of motivation for them to get to the next level.

At any rate, the response to the brochure was overwhelmingly positive, based on surveys sent to a sampling of officers after the brochure went out.

### What Not to Include in Compensation Communications

You don't need to include photos or videos of the head of HR or the head of Compensation in your compensation communications. Why? It's kind of like trying to sell a car with videos of the engineers who designed it. What excites them about the vehicle may or may not excite the potential buyer, who doesn't need to know all the exciting terms and functions of the parts under the hood.

You also don't need to include empty language or jargon, such as this:

- "Our people represent our greatest long-term sustainable asset." In fact, avoid starting sentences with the phrase "Our people represent. . ." It's way too lofty, not conversational, hard to read, and difficult to reconcile with the reality of work today. Someone reading the "Our people. . ." platitudes will do a rewrite for you that goes something like this: "Our people are fabulous, until they're not, and then we get rid of them."
- "To achieve our goals, we need extraordinarily talented leaders and a world-class rewards program to match."

If you decide to feature senior managers talking about the goals of the compensation program, include quotes from them in a conversational tone. One of our favorites quotes from the CEO of a financial firm is "If making a lot of money is the only reason you're here, we're probably not the right company for you." He went on to describe why the caliber of the people you work with, what you learn, and the work you'll do should be important enough reasons to race into work each day. It was a great way to put pay in its proper place for that firm.

## Create Visuals to Simplify Complicated Information

You've never needed visuals (see Chapter 6, "Leverage Visuals") more than when you set out to communicate compensation. After all, you're dealing with three attributes that lend themselves to a visual treatment: numbers, relationships (how an aspect of performance affects pay, for instance), and time.

The easiest visual to use is a table. For example, here's one we created for a compensation guide for managers at a biotech company:

*Overview: Calculating Bonus Compensation*

|  | Aspect 1 | Aspect 2 | Aspect 3 |
|---|---|---|---|
| **Overview** | The employee's band and salary determine the **bonus potential**. | The employee's final performance rating gives you a guideline for the **bonus recommendation**. | To tie company performance to individual rewards, the **bonus recommendation** is multiplied by the **corporate performance multiplier (CPM)**, which may increase or decrease the employee's final bonus amount. |
| **How to Calculate** | band % × salary = bonus potential | bonus potential % recommendation for rating = bonus recommendation | bonus recommendation × corporate performance multiplier = final bonus amount |
| **More Details** | See page 9 | See page 11 | See page 12 |

Here are two more examples of how visuals can create clarity about aspects of compensation. Figure 14-1 illustrates a company's new career ladder, showing the job bands or levels that determine the pay range for a set of jobs.

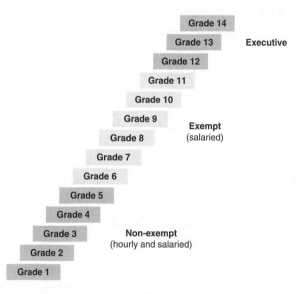

**Figure 14-1    Career ladder**

Figure 14-2 illustrates a change in a pay cycle—when employees will receive an annual bonus.

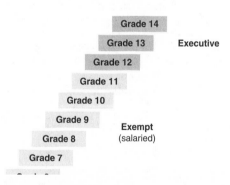

**Figure 14-2    Pay cycle change**

## Help Prepare Managers to Talk About Pay

Critical information about an employee's pay—such as salary increases and bonus amounts—usually is communicated to that employee in a one-on-one conversation with his or her manager. Especially when compensation is complex, or when the system is changing, it's essential that you prepare managers for success by giving them the context and information they need to speak confidently and persuasively about pay.

Helping managers usually begins with making sure they understand the process. For example, here's a checklist Alison's firm created for a manager's guide to compensation for a global company:

**What you need to do:**

By September 1 of this year, you'll need to have a year-end conversation with each of your employees to discuss their final rating and compensation. Ideally, salary and bonus information is communicated in an individual face-to-face meeting with an employee.

**Share the following information with *all* employees:**

✓ Tell the employee his or her final rating for the previous plan year.

✓ Communicate the salary increase amount. If no salary increase was awarded, share the reasons why, and describe what needs to occur for the employee to be considered for future increases.

✓ Give specific developmental feedback to help the employee improve, grow, and/or add new skills.

✓ Reinforce the employee's goals for the new plan year.

**Share additional information with bonus-eligible employees:**

✓ Communicate the bonus amount, and reinforce why the bonus is being granted.

✓ Describe how the employee's role and performance contributed to the company's success.

✓ Explain how the company and business unit met or exceeded performance indicators and how this impacts all bonuses in the Corporate Performance Multiplier. Detailed information about this is included in the previous section, "What you need to know about bonuses."

✓ If no bonus was awarded, share the reasons why, and describe what needs to occur for the employee to be considered for future bonus awards.

✓ Thank the employee for his or her work in achieving corporate and business unit objectives.

When we helped a client roll out a new sales incentive plan, we learned that typically the client simply announced the new plan each year at the national sales meeting. Company management perceived, and our research confirmed, that the sales staff's understanding of the new plan was highly uneven, which was translating into lost sales for the company, plus lower sales bonuses for employees.

Our approach was to use a variety of communications and tools, both before and after the national sales meeting, to engage sales managers in the process, give them a variety of tools, and provide "just in time" information rather than bombarding them with all the materials for a one-year campaign at one time.

This approach worked wonders. Sales went up significantly, as did the average bonus payout.

Here's an overview of what happened before and after the national sales meeting:

| At this time: | Here's what sales managers do or receive: |
|---|---|
| 2 weeks before | Attend a web training session to prepare them to host district-level training breakouts of the sales meeting. |
| 10 days before | Receive kits with additional materials, including speaker's notes with guidance on how to highlight specifics and takeaways on each slide. |
| 1 week before | Take an online self-assessment that tests their knowledge of the sales compensation program and how prepared they are to answer questions about the program. |
| At the national sales meeting | Hold district-level breakout sessions to review the sales compensation program with their teams. |

| At this time: | Here's what sales managers do or receive: |
|---|---|
| 1 week after | Receive a FAQ document that answers the most commonly asked questions about the sales compensation program. |
| 2 weeks after | Receive a flipbook tabletop training easel. New pages are provided each month so that sales managers can use the tool at meetings to highlight high performers and provide tips on how to maximize bonus earnings. |

## Personalize if Possible

About 40 years ago, companies began producing what they called total compensation reports: a personalized communication showing an employee the cumulative value of his or her job. Somewhere in the report you found a grand total that added up the value of your vacation time, sick days, holidays, medical coverage, plus, of course, your pay.

The early reports were not beautiful to look at—and when you saw a lot of white space, you knew that someone, somewhere was probably getting something terrific and you were not. For example, when the page about Supplemental Compensation featured one tiny sentence and the rest was white space, you knew you were, essentially, a bottom feeder.

These early reports were extremely popular and extremely expensive to produce. As technology caught up with need, the reports became seamless—filled with lots of details and no telltale white space to signal a void in your life.

Today's reports don't even need to be printed. Many organizations provide employees with confidential online access to the same information in the total compensation report—and more. Employees can use modeling tools to make their own assumptions and projections. For saving and investing purposes, these new tools are an important resource to help employees make good decisions and take actions so that they will have the income they would like to have at retirement, or if they were to stop working.

Of course, many companies still need to produce printed total compensation reports for many reasons—for example, if many employees don't have access to online resources. If your organization does produce a printed report, we recommend that you also mail it to employees at home. The report contains the type of information that employees will want to share with their families, because it serves as an important document for financial planning.

Here's an overview of the types of information you can include in a total compensation report:

- Salary plus any incentive pay or awards
- Company investments in 401(k) or similar plans or any matching gifts
- Company investment in the benefits package
- Medical and dental reimbursements for the past year, plus what the company paid and the employee paid for this coverage, plus a summary of coverage (deductible, copay, out-of-pocket maximum)
- A reminder of how the healthcare spending account can save money (if the employee doesn't currently take advantage of it)
- Projected tax savings based on the amount the employee contributes to the healthcare spending account
- An overview of projected financial support from various sources if the employee became disabled or died
- An overview of paid time off and its value
- An overview of any additional services the company provides to help employees get assistance with personal problems, find information on family care, spend more time with their families, invest in others (matching-gifts programs), and invest in themselves (for example, tuition reimbursement). Be sure to show the actual dollar amounts for any applicable programs.
- Show current and projected values for any retirement savings accounts. Include information that will help employees determine if they need to increase their savings, and by how much, to have more at retirement. (And include instructions on how to do just that.) Include estimated social security monthly payments for different possible retirement ages. Give employees

information about what percentage of their salaries they'll need during retirement to continue their current standard of living.

• Whenever you present information that may cause an employee to take action, make it easy for him to do just that. Include a link to the appropriate website or a toll-free phone number.

Here's the introduction to a printed total compensation report called "Pay Plus" that Jane produced:

Dear Employee,

Our success starts with people like you. One of the important benefits that all of us share is our total compensation package: salary, incentives and awards, and benefits.

That's what this booklet is all about. It describes your total compensation package in a form that's completely customized for you. For example, you'll see a report on your earnings, including the value of your benefits. You'll find a summary of your benefit choices and some tips on how to get more from the programs offered to you. There's even a section on long-term financial planning. It's designed to help you determine whether your current level of savings will meet your future needs.

You might be wondering why we've invested in this statement. It's because we believe it will help you become more informed about your total compensation and how to use your benefits to meet your life needs and goals. The statement gives you a new tool for making financial decisions and planning for the future. And, it may provide you with a new perspective on your compensation and the ways we can share success.

[signed by the chairman of the company]

How did we measure the effectiveness of this report? We included a one-page survey for employees to complete and return anonymously. The survey included questions such as the following, each followed by a four-point scale moving from Strongly Disagree on the left to Strongly Agree on the right:

• The personal statement improves my understanding of my total compensation.

- The personal statement improves my appreciation of the value of my total compensation.
- Based on my understanding, I am getting as much value out of the total compensation plan as I can.
- Based on my understanding, I plan to reevaluate how I'm using certain benefits in order to get more out of them.
- I intend to increase my current level of savings in order to meet my financial goals.

Then we included one opportunity for comments:

- What's the single most important improvement the company can make in the personal total compensation statement? Any other comments?

Survey results proved overwhelmingly that this report was a good investment.

## *Provide Examples*

Even if your company doesn't produce a personalized compensation/benefits statement, you can make compensation more tangible for managers and employees. How? By providing examples of how pay works. One easy way to do so is to create semifictional characters and then illustrate what happens to them as a result of different pay events.

For example, we created the character of "Michael" so that managers at a healthcare company would understand how salary increases and bonuses work:

**Meet Michael**

Michael is a Band 4 employee with an annual salary of $50,000. He just received a "strong" rating for his performance last year.

**Band and salary determine bonus potential**

As a Band 4, Michael's bonus potential is 15% of his annual salary. Since his salary is $50,000, this means his bonus potential is $7,500.

### Final rating determines bonus recommendation

Since Michael's final rating is "strong," the guideline for his bonus recommendation is between 81% and 90% of his bonus potential, with a midpoint of 86%. At the midpoint, his bonus recommendation would be $6,450, or 12.9% of his salary.

Since Michael performed well on an important project that helped increase revenue, his manager recommends him for a slightly higher bonus of $6,600, which is 88% of his bonus potential and 13.2% of his annual salary.

Michael's bonus recommendation is reviewed and approved by his second-level manager in the calibration process.

See how this example helps bring pay to life?

# Checklist for Getting Value from Your Substantial Investment in Compensation

To make sure your compensation communications succeed, you'll want to do the following:

✓ Use simple, clear, conversational language to talk about pay. This isn't brain surgery. It doesn't require technical terms that only a compensation professional could love.

✓ Produce visuals to show how components add up and work together. Graphs create a succinct, easy-to-understand picture.

✓ Create ways for employees to see how the value of everything the company provides really does add up.

✓ Give employees information that helps them make good long-term plans.

✓ Go the extra mile to give managers "just in time" information to help them talk effectively one-on-one or in small groups about pay and incentive plans.

# 15 — Performance Management

*In this chapter, you learn how to*

- *Communicate your company's goals so employees can set their performance objectives to help the company succeed*
- *Create understanding about how your performance management system works*
- *Develop communication tools that simplify performance management*
- *Provide help for managers so that they can fulfill their guiding, coaching, and feedback roles*

## It's Report Card Time!

If you were a straight-A student, you probably looked forward to receiving every report card. But some of us were easily distracted by boys or baseball or hairstyles or Hendrix. We did well in some subjects (hello, English!) but struggled through others (geometry should be outlawed). So we dreaded report card time. We had trouble even opening the envelope. We walked home from school the long way. And when it was time to show Dad, we closed our eyes and waited for the lecture about "not realizing your potential" to be over.

Unfortunately, when it's time to meet with their manager about their performance appraisal, employees can suffer a painful flashback to report card time. After all, performance reviews don't just determine grade point average; they affect how an employee is paid, whether he gets a promotion, and even whether he keeps his job.

It's no wonder that employees, managers, and even HR professionals view performance management as a challenge. In fact, a poll released at a Conference Board talent-management event in March 2010 found that 72% of responders portrayed performance management as "an endless struggle in which they were neither gaining nor losing ground." Ten percent declared that "the war for talent was winding down in defeat for their enterprise." And a 2004 Watson Wyatt survey found that just 30% of employees believed that their company's performance management systems actually improved their performance.

But wait—there's more bad news. The consequences of poorly executed performance management are dramatic:

- Loss of trust between employee and manager (and management in general)
- Low employee morale and engagement
- Attrition of talented people
- Lack of direction for the organization as a whole
- Poor employee performance and missed company objectives

Fortunately, there's hope. Of course, we believe that the key to performance management is communication. So we show you how to communicate about performance management so that everyone understands the company's direction, so that managers and employees know how the performance management system works, and so that they're set up to succeed at using the system to contribute to company success.

# What Is Performance Management?

Let's start by sharing our definition of "performance management": a system of defining the employee's job, setting annual objectives that describe what the employee will focus on, and evaluating how well the employee performed. The idea is to create a positive environment that allows people to perform at a consistently high level. It includes the following elements:

- Understanding the company's culture, philosophy, and strategy
- Setting objectives based on company and group goals
- Receiving ongoing coaching and feedback from your manager, along with having regular performance discussions
- Being recognized and compensated according to how well you perform your job and meet your goals
- Learning and improving through training and development

As you can see, an annual performance review—which is just one meeting—does not equal performance management. Performance management is also not the same as "talent management," an HR term that serves as an umbrella for recruiting, staffing, performance management, organizational development, and succession planning. For our purposes, we focus on performance management and how it relates to the individual employee, not teams or financial or business performance.

# What Do Employees Want?

We always like to keep in mind why employees care about performance management. Employees want answers to a universal set of questions:

- Am I doing the right things to help the company and advance my career?

- How am I performing compared to my peers?
- Do I have a future with this company?
- How do I get better at what I do?

# Begin with Company Goals

How can employees do their jobs to support company success? How do they set objectives that make a difference to company performance? These are important questions, and the answer begins with making sure employees understand what the company wants to accomplish.

This seems so fundamental that we're surprised that many companies don't take the time to articulate company objectives in a simple, clear way that every employee can understand. You may have a complicated strategic plan that a management consultant helped senior leaders develop. That's great, but that plan is probably too detailed (and maybe too confidential) to share. What you're looking for is something straightforward that expresses what your company is trying to accomplish this year in key categories such as these:

- **Financial.**   What are your sales, profitability, and other financial goals?
- **New products or services.**   Are you launching new products or expanding brands? Trying to acquire new clients or enter new markets?
- **Initiatives.**   What big projects do you need to complete?
- **People.**   Have you set overall objectives for how you hire, retain, and develop people?
- **Other issues.**   Maybe you have an environmental goal, a community relations goal, or some other area that matters to your company.

## How We Articulate Our Goals

Alison's company (Davis & Company) has developed a simple page that articulates what the firm will try to accomplish in a given year. Figure 15-1 shows the 2010 version.

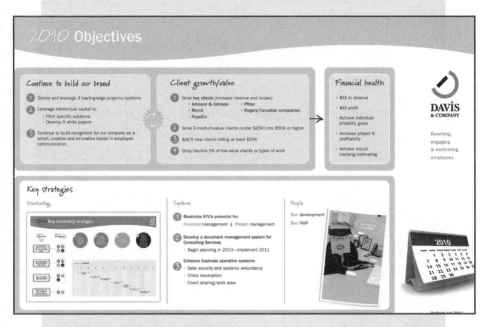

**Figure 15-1 Company objectives**

We present this page at a staff meeting early in January and spend time discussing it so that everyone understands what we're trying to accomplish. Then each employee works with his or her manager to set individual goals. We consider ourselves lucky. We're a small company, so it's relatively simple to connect what an employee does to what the company wants to achieve; the degree of separation is not very great.

# Connecting the Dots if Your Company Is Large

If you have a large company, you need to work harder to manage the flow of objectives from the company level down to the individual level. The challenge is to make priorities meaningful for employees by connecting the dots so that employees have a clear line of sight. They need to be able to see the links from organizational goals, to divisional priorities, to group/team focus areas, down to an employee's individual objectives.

At a large financial services firm, senior management had long been successful at setting priorities at a company level. But the company had not brought those goals to life for managers and their teams. So several years ago, HR set out to provide managers with the tools they needed to communicate with their employees about how those priorities connected to and were supported by team and individual goals.

HR gathered information about priorities from each of the business units and created a tool to help leaders and managers share them with employees. The tool was divided into thirds:

| On the left, five company objectives were listed. | The middle section listed three to five division, plant, or business unit objectives. | The right section was left blank so that the department manager could discuss which of the company and regional objectives apply to his or her team and then fill in department objectives or even individual objectives. |
|---|---|---|

To help managers understand what to do, HR invited managers to attend a web workshop (scheduled at different times of day so that managers could choose the time that worked best for them). There they were briefed on the objectives of the effort and setting expectations and were instructed in the use of the objectives tool.

Manager feedback about the process was positive. Ninety-nine percent of managers agreed that they understood the importance of talking to their team about priorities, and 86% agreed that they had a better understanding of how to discuss priorities with their team. Here are some sample comments:

- "Great class! It really helped to understand where the bank as a whole was coming from and how to break down to employee level. I would attend this again."
- "This workshop was very informative and motivating. I do intend to apply the strategies mentioned in an upcoming meeting. Thank you."

# Does Everyone Understand Your Performance Management System?

We're big fans of simple performance management systems, because they're easy for managers and employees to use. For example, Davis & Company has developed a straightforward goal-setting process that starts with company objectives. Sometimes (but not always) it includes a team goal. Then it asks the manager and employee to develop objectives in two categories:

- Performance goals (what an employee will focus on in his or her job this year to support company success)
- Development goals (one or two ways in which an employee will improve his or her skills)

## Lorraine's Performance Management Plan

Lorraine Fabiano is our Finance and HR director. (We're a small company, so she has two roles.) Figure 15-2 shows her individual performance management plan for 2010. (Yes, that's it; it fits on part of a page.)

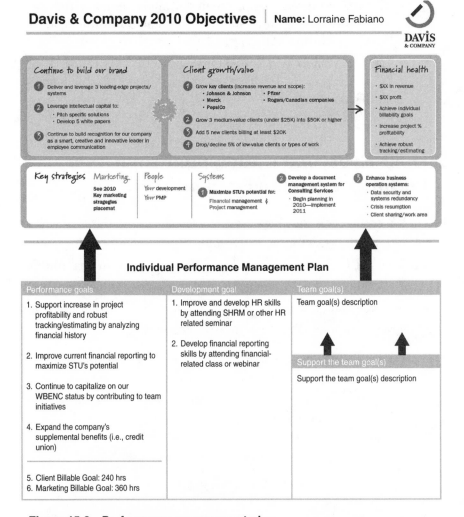

Figure 15-2    Performance management plan

CHAPTER 15 • PERFORMANCE MANAGEMENT

# What if Your System Is Complicated?

If your performance management system is more complex, you need to work harder to make sure that employees understand how it operates. Don't assume that just because you've had the system for a while that everybody gets it.

A couple of years ago, we worked with a pharmaceutical company to communicate new online tools for performance management. The idea was that the tools—such as one to record your goals and another for managers to rate your performance—hadn't changed, just the way you fill them out had. But when we interviewed managers, we learned that even experienced managers weren't sure they were completing the forms correctly. We used this feedback to develop a guidebook called "Using the Ratings and Appraisal Tool: A Guide for Managers."

The guide was focused on giving managers step-by-step instructions for using the online tool, but we also subtly included lots of tips that would help managers remember how to do a better job of performance management. For example, the introduction included this advice:

**Preparing Performance Appraisals**

Your candid and constructive feedback in the Performance Appraisal is one of the key drivers of employee performance. In preparing the appraisals, you should take into account:

- Development and performance coaching conversations you have had with each employee throughout the year
- Your observations of the employee's performance and relative contribution
- Feedback from others who have observed the employee's performance and relative contribution
- The employee's self-assessment

And here's a typical tip we included:

**Tip**

You'll notice that if the employee has submitted a self-assessment, the employee's comments for each objective appear in the Self-Assessment Column. If you don't see comments from the employee, check to determine if he or she plans to submit a self-assessment.

# The Big Picture

Such specific instruction is helpful, but it's also important to help managers and employees understand how the entire performance management system works. Particularly important are the intersections between performance management and development (especially if they're separate systems, as is the case at many companies) and performance management and pay. (See Chapter 14, "Compensation," for more on communicating about compensation.)

This doesn't mean burdening employees with all the behind-the-scenes details you manage in HR. A few years ago, we worked on a project with an HR team charged with changing the performance management system to support the company's direction. Unfortunately, this team was so fascinated by the intricacies of their system that they felt it was necessary to communicate the entire contents of the system. They included the kitchen sink, plus everything from the refrigerator, the cabinets, and the laundry room.

"We need people to see the big picture," said the head of the team. "I think your approach is too simplistic. I've come up with something more comprehensive." It's shown in Figure 15-3.

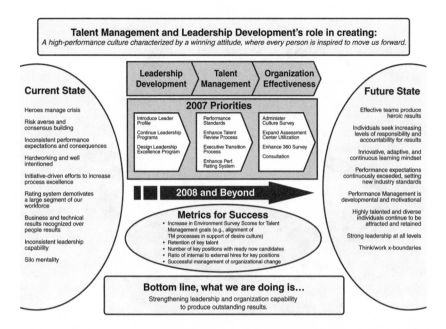

**Figure 15-3   A complicated talent management and leadership development diagram**

"Nooooo!" (You can hear our scream from way over there, can't you?) This poor team was sadly misguided. Their hearts were pure, but they were so in love with their work that they wanted to make the system more intricate than it actually was.

Contrast the scary diagram shown in Figure 15-3 with the simple depiction of a performance management process shown in Figure 15-4.

Nice, isn't it? This company operates on a fiscal year, so an important component of all its communication about performance management is time. The company constantly reminds employees that its performance cycle follows its business cycle, so it's not on a calendar year basis.

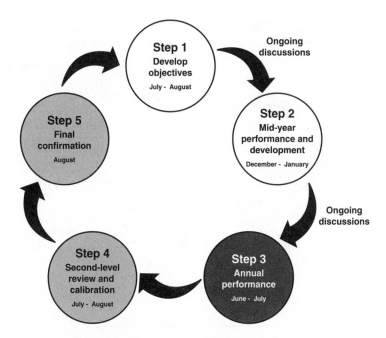

**Figure 15-4    A simple performance management diagram**

Another company wanted to show the timeline in relation to how the company set goals. Figure 15-5 shows how its system was illustrated.

The Performance and Development planning process is a critical business process aligned with and grounded in R&D business planning. R&D's overall performance is the collection of our individual results.

| Business Planning and Alignment* | | | | Performance and Dev't Planning | Performance and Dev't Discussions | Formal Performance Evaluation |
|---|---|---|---|---|---|---|
| Portfolio and projects align with R&D strategy | Matrix and project teams determine their requirements | Lines determine business goals based on matrix and project requirements | Lines cascade business goals to individuals | Individuals establish PAOs, HPB targets, and create individual development plans | Collect evidence and course correct through:<br>• Objective evidence<br>• Stakeholder feedback<br>• Ongoing discussions | Evaluate performance input from multiple sources:<br>• What (job duties + PAOs)<br>• How (HPBs + culture) |
| OCT | NOV | DEC | JAN | JAN | ◀ ONGOING ▶ | DEC |

\* Timing may vary based on business requirements

**Figure 15-5    Performance and development planning and evaluation timeline**

What if you can use only words to communicate your performance management process? Here are some key messages that describe changes to a complex program:

## Changes to the Performance Management System designed to help each employee reach his or her potential

**What is changing:**

Beginning in January, employees will experience changes to Performance Management processes:

- A new system for **Performance Ratings**, as part of the **Performance Management Process**, will affect how employees set goals for the year, how they're appraised on achieving those goals, how they're rated, and how their managers determine year-end bonuses and merit increases.

- These changes are based on a new set of criteria called **Leadership Qualities**, designed to provide a framework for the attributes that every employee needs to achieve in order to help the company succeed.

**Who is affected:**

Every employee who participates in the Performance Management process and is eligible for a bonus and a merit increase will experience these changes during the year.

**When changes are occurring:**

Beginning in the first quarter of the year, when employees work with their managers to set their goals for the year.

**Why these changes are being made:**

The company's past success has come from hard work and the ability to anticipate and adapt to a changing marketplace. But the past is no guarantee of future success. That's why over the past few years, the company has looked closely at every aspect of our business. And that effort has paid off. We've found innovative, better, more efficient, more productive ways to do things, while maintaining or improving quality and effectiveness.

One area we've been looking at is the way we attract, retain, develop, and reward our employees. It's clear that people are critical to the company's success. Yet many of our Performance Management systems are many years old. Other systems work well in parts of our organization but are not leveraged across the company globally.

The goal of efforts to improve our Performance Management and Development System is clear: to set up every employee for success. That means clear, consistent expectations for what employees need to do in their jobs. And making sure employees are rewarded and recognized for their smart thinking and hard work. And managing talent so that the right employees are in the right roles across the organization.

**What is *not* changing:**

For most of the organization, the Performance Management Process itself will not change. Employees will still work with their manager to set goals, conduct a self-assessment, receive a performance appraisal and a rating, and be compensated accordingly. What's changing is how employees set goals based on a new appraisal and rating system and how bonuses and merit increases are determined.

# Teaching Managers to Fish

Almost every performance management system relies heavily on managers to make it work. Managers help employees set goals, they provide ongoing and periodic feedback, they evaluate performance, and they make recommendations on how employees will be paid. So our final piece of advice about communication performance is this: Invest in managers.

That usually means using multiple channels to teach managers to be good at performance management: training (in person or online), web tools, print pieces, even peer networks.

In fact, this is one of those topics that benefits from realizing that every time you communicate with managers, you have the opportunity to provide a little training, too.

For example, when a global company was rolling out a new performance management system that would give managers improved online tools, we recommended using videos of managers from around the world as part of the managers' tool kit on the company intranet.

Specifically, we recommended the company identify high-potential, highly respected managers to be videotaped (using inexpensive FLIP cameras) answering questions such as these:

- What's the best advice you ever received from a boss?
- How do you recommend dealing with problem employees?
- How did you turn around an employee's poor performance?

The resulting footage could be shared with managers throughout the company in a variety of ways: webinars, training sessions, and online training.

For another global company we created a comprehensive guide for managers that included these sections:

- President's message
- Overview of Performance Management
- Roles and responsibilities
- A quick-start guide for Performance Management
  Step 1: Develop objectives
  Step 2: Mid-year performance and development
  Step 3: Annual performance
  Step 4: Second-level review and calibration
  Step 5: Final confirmation
- Frequently Asked Questions

One of the first sections in the guidebook was a description of the manager's role:

Within Performance Management you are responsible for coordinating work across your team, and coaching and assessing your performance. To do this, you need to:

- Help your employee understand the company group, functional and site objectives, and how your team's work aligns with those objectives
- Distribute key objectives for the year among team members

- Support the employee as he sets his career goals and creates a development plan

- Work with each employee to assess her performance at mid-year and year-end and determine her performance rating

- Provide recognition, feedback, and coaching throughout the year to help the employee achieve individual and overall objectives

Here is how we described the importance of mid-year reviews:

Open communication and ongoing feedback and development are essential to effective performance management. The mid-year assessment and development plan is an opportunity to make sure this happens effectively. You and your employee have a shared responsibility to monitor the employee's progress in achieving objectives, including what is being achieved, how it is being achieved, and the overall impact on the business. Identify any potential barriers—and possible solutions—to make sure the employee achieves his objectives and completes his development plan. There should be no surprises during the formal reviews.

## Help Managers Know What Really Improves Performance

In an article titled, "An Alternative to Performance Appraisal," in the June 2010 issue of *HR Magazine*, Erik Van Slyke explains why performance management processes often don't get desired results, and he identifies what managers can do to improve performance:

"It's amazing to think that 45 years after the *Harvard Business Review* published 'Split Roles in Performance Appraisal' (Myer, Kay, & French), we still believe performance appraisal works. The study, conducted at GE, found that the company's performance management system not only didn't work, it produced results that were the opposite of what was intended:

Criticism has a negative impact on goals and praise had little effect one way or another.

"Countless other scientific studies have arrived at similar conclusions. And more powerfully, research conducted with brain scanning technologies...have shown that these results are directly connected to the way the brain works.

"So what works? What generates higher levels of performance? The most effective and sustainable solution for improving performance is intrinsic motivation. High performance comes when people love what they do. And while managers may seem to have little ability to directly affect intrinsic motivation, they can create an environment that draws out and inspires it."

# Checklist for Communicating Performance Management

✓ Communicate your company's goals so that employees understand where you're going and what they can do to help.

✓ Connect the dots (if your company is large) so that employees have a line of sight between their job and the big picture.

✓ Determine if a visual will help you illustrate how your performance management system works.

✓ Use plain language to explain even the most complex performance management system.

✓ Invest in managers. Make sure they have what they need to coach their employees through the performance management process.

✓ Treat every communication opportunity as a training opportunity. Make sure you give managers plenty of tips on how to give performance feedback effectively.

# 16

## Saving for Retirement

*In this chapter, you learn how to*

- *Encourage employees to save for tomorrow*
- *Share information that helps employees make good investment decisions*
- *Increase employee participation in savings and stock plans*

## Hey, Can We Get Some Help Over Here?

We're lucky: We love our work. Usually, we trundle along without thinking too much about it, but the other day Alison got a call from a young man pursuing his Ph.D. in communication who wanted to interview her as part of his research.

"Sure!" she said.

One of his questions was this: "What about your work gives you the most satisfaction?"

Easy, she replied. "I love the fact that when communication works well, employees understand an issue, know what it means to them, see clearly what they need to do, and feel like someone cared enough to help them. What could be cooler than that?"

We mention this because when it comes to saving for retirement, employees need our (and your) help. We know (from personal experience) that challenging economic times have made it more difficult for people to save for and manage their retirement. But we are still dismayed by the high percentage of employees who are in serious trouble. For example, a 2010 study by the Employee Benefit Research Institute found the following:[1]

- Only 16% of workers say they are very confident they have enough money to retire. Forty-six percent are not too confident or not at all confident that they will have enough money to live comfortably when they retire.
- 27% of current employees have less than $1,000 in savings, and 54% have less than $25,000.
- Almost two-thirds of Americans at lower income levels will run short of money after 10 years of retirement.

All these facts add to our conviction that one of your most important goals should be to increase employee participation in your company's 401(k), other retirement savings plans, and stock plans. You want to go the extra mile to create effective HR communication that

- Educates employees on the importance of saving for tomorrow
- Increases participation in retirement and stock plan savings
- Shares information that will help employees make good investment choices

Effective communication can mean the difference between a comfortable retirement and a difficult one. Helping employees with investing can mean that they will have money to buy homes, improve the home they have, invest in their children's education, and live comfortably after they stop working. You can actually help people build a financially secure future. It's an incredibly powerful gift!

So let's get started.

# You're Ready for Your Simple Four-Step Program!

Here are four techniques that work to increase employee participation in savings or stock or retirement plans:

1. Simply and clearly explain how financial stuff works. (Don't assume that even the most sophisticated employees are financially literate.)

2. Use a how-to, "service journalism" (see Chapter 5, "Write Simply and Clearly") approach to communicating about retirement by giving employees information they can use.

3. Create video (or print) "stories" of employees describing how they have benefited from the plan. Show them on screens in lobbies and cafeterias or on the company intranet.

4. Personalize if possible. Your retirement plan service provider may offer the option to provide personalized statements in print or online. Take advantage of that option, but also consider supplementing those statements to make a strong point.

# Not Algebra, But . . .

In the 1986 movie *Peggy Sue Got Married*, Peggy Sue (played by Kathleen Turner) goes to her high school reunion, faints, and then wakes up back in high school—*except* that she's retained 20 years of memories.

Her knowledge of the future provides many funny lines. One of our favorites is a remark to her math teacher: "Well, Mr. Snelgrove, I happen to know that in the future I will not have the slightest use for algebra, and I speak from experience."

We feel precisely the same way (about algebra), but it turns out that Peggy Sue was wrong about one thing: It is helpful to understand math well enough to make smart financial choices.

## Stock Options 101

Not all of us paid attention in math class—and many employees have never been educated about the financial market. So a key communication strategy is to explain patiently and clearly what investment choices are and how they work.

A pharmaceutical company made changes to its long-term incentive program to make it more advantageous to the leaders and managers who were eligible to participate. Alison's team knew from interviewing a sample of these participants that many felt uncomfortable with some of the options. They admitted to us (privately) that they felt they should be knowledgeable about these financial instruments, but quite frankly were not.

So when we communicated the changes, we made sure to cover the basics. For example, here is what we wrote about one aspect of the incentive program:

### About Stock Options

| | |
|---|---|
| What they are | The right to purchase a set number of shares of company stock at a fixed price for a specific period of time. |
| Why they're valuable | An option generates value to you if the market price of stock is higher than the grant price when you're ready to exercise (buy) your options.<br><br>(However, if the market price falls below or stays the same as the grant price, the option has no value and would not be exercised.) |
| Vesting | Stock options vest in increments of one-third of granted options (33/13%) each year for three years after being granted. Once your options vest, you may exercise them at any time up to 10 years from the original date of the grant. |
| Example | An employee is granted 100 stock options at $40 per share. Three years later, all the options have vested, and the market price of company stock is $44. The employee decides to exercise the options, which means that he buys the 100 shares of stock at a price that is $4 lower than the current market price. That's a profit of $4 per share, or $400. |

# How to Get Smarter and Richer

As we describe in Chapter 5, one of the most compelling kinds of information is the kind that helps you solve a problem or improve your life. That's why recipes are so appealing, or HGTV, or even just the words "how to."

Since many of us struggle to understand complex financial issues, we especially appreciate gentle "here's how" information provided to help us make good decisions about our investments or retirement program.

For a financial services company, Jane took advantage of the requirement to provide employees with an annual report of their savings incentive plan. She turned that communication into a "marketing" brochure that included these sections in this order:

- Eight reasons to save and invest
- Seven steps to sound investment decisions
- An overview of plan features, transactions, and funds
- How your investments performed
- Investment fund portfolios (showing how each fund was invested)

Understanding that many employees skim over print or online communications, she made sure every headline and subhead did some heavy lifting. She used them to tell a story, too, so if all a reader did was glance at the first two sections of this brochure, here's what he would see:

**Eight reasons to save and invest:**

- Double your award
- Cut your tax bill every time you invest
- Earn investment income now; pay taxes later
- Small, regular investments add up
- Choose the investments you prefer

- It's not just for retirement
- It's never too soon
- You *can* take it with you

We think at least one of these subheads would draw in the reader to learn more.

Here again is simple, brief advice on how to invest in yourself:

**Seven steps to sound investment decisions:**

1. Understand risk
2. Know your time horizon
3. Understand yourself
4. Study your finances
5. Evaluate the plan funds
6. Diversify
7. Reevaluate your plan periodically

# How to Give Advice When You Can't Give Advice

To give employees information that helps them make sound investment decisions, we use language such as "Experts agree . . ." or "Most financial advisors would recommend. . . ." Or we cite actual facts, figures, and historical performance that can help employees make good decisions.

You need to repeat good financial investment advice every time you communicate about stock and savings plans, because for at least some of your readers, this is "just in time" information. They're new to the company or have decided to participate in the plan for the first time, so you need to repeat the information that will continue to help them make good decisions.

Here's how we described making investment choices in the summary plan description of a company's 401(k) plan:

You'll want to consider your personal financial goals, review fund performance over time, learn about the different funds, and then pick your investments. No one employed by the company can give you advice about how to invest.

Most people who invest hope to increase the value of their savings over time. Most financial advisors explain to investors the value of diversification: selecting several different funds to invest in.

You can choose from a number of funds, including a stable value fund as well as mutual funds, or you can select one of the [Special] funds, which are asset allocation mutual funds that automatically diversify your investments based on when you anticipate receiving the money in your account at retirement.

On a following two-page spread, the nine available funds were described, moving from low-risk/low-reward to high-risk/high-reward funds. The headings were

Name of Fund:

Goal:

Invests in:

Designed for:

Here's the text for the Stable Value fund:

**Goal:** To preserve your principal investment while earning interest income. The fund will try to maintain a stable $1 unit price.

**Invests in:** Investment contracts, offered by major insurers and financial institutions, and certain types of fixed-income securities that pay interest at a specified rate.

**Designed for:** Someone who wants a slightly higher yield than money market funds, or someone interested in price stability to balance other, more aggressive investments.

This text uses simple language, combined with concise summaries that describe what the fund invests in and who it is designed for. The reader gets a complete picture that will help her decide which funds to invest in. She can even figure out how to use one fund to balance an investment in a more high-risk/high-reward fund.

# "Tell Me How You Got to Be So Rich"

Real stories about real employees are one of the most credible and effective ways you can persuade more employees to take advantage of savings or stock plans.

We've shared this advice many times throughout this book, and this is one topic where real stories shared by real employees make a huge difference.

For a brochure on retirement savings, Jane featured photographs of and quotes from 21 employees—both male and female, with diverse ages and jobs, from a variety of the company's locations in the U.S. Even if you read only the photo captions, you got a great overview of plan features and benefits—and incentives to sign up. Here are some examples of how effective real people with real stories can be at increasing employee participation in a savings plan:

"Two aspects of the plan really appeal to me: the tax-deferred status and the many choices of investment funds. I plan to use the money I'm saving to buy a house."
*Wayne, New York*


"What attracted me was the fact that the company matches my basic award 100% if I save and invest it. It's both an incentive and an opportunity to save for the future."
*Eli, San Antonio*

"The plan provides an interesting way to prepare for retirement that I don't believe exists in my home country, Japan. The plan makes it effortless to save and get tax savings at the same time."

*Mayumi, New York*


"The moment you sign up to save and invest, you're an instant winner since the company matches your basic award. (In Las Vegas, we like instant winners!) With this plan, [company name] shows its support for employees in concrete terms. This is an investment in your future."

*Carlos, Las Vegas*


"I encourage all my employees to participate actively. It's a wonderful benefit to help employees save for retirement, because you're never too young to start thinking about retirement."

*Geri, San Francisco*


"I'm contributing extra money each paycheck because they take the money out, I don't see it, and it's going to a good cause—me. It's a good way to save. I'm saving for a down payment on a house."

*Joseph, New York*


"It's so hard to put money away these days. This plan makes it easy. Plus, it gives me security to know I have the money if I need it in an emergency. I also like the fact that I can change my investments each month."

*Shelley, Sioux Falls*

# More Stories

For a stock purchase plan, we summarized the entire plan on the cover of a print piece using an illustration of a diverse group of employees. Eight of them made these comments, reading left to right:

- "Buying stocks seems pretty confusing to me."
- "I just filed my tax return. I'm an expert on confusion. This plan seems pretty simple to me."
- "I agree. Knowing you can buy stock at a fixed price any time during two years is easy to understand."
- "I think it's a good deal—your money earns interest while you're saving to buy stock."
- "I'm a Libra. I hate decisions. This plan offers two kinds of stock—which should I buy?"
- "You can decide to buy book value or market value, some of both, or none at all. Best of all, you can change your mind for a full *two* years."
- "Opinions are fine, but I want *facts* before I decide to invest in stocks. How do I find out more?"
- "It's verrrrrry simple. Turn the page. Just turn the page."

We continued to use illustrations on each spread of this brochure. We showed how two employees from the company used the plan in different ways and how both were satisfied with the results after two years.

# When You're Announcing a New Plan, Write Your Own Story

But what if you don't have employee stories to tell? When you're introducing something new, you can't draw upon people's experiences. That's why, when we introduced a new stock purchase plan for all employees, we created our own story.

Research showed that most employees in this company were scared to invest in the stock market—even in the stock of the company they worked for. People at the lower ends of the salary scale simply did not view themselves as "stockholders"—that was only for wealthy people.

So we created a man who was afraid of a lot of things, and illustrator Edward Sorel brought him to life. "Once I was afraid," he says in the caption of the first full-page illustration. "Afraid of tall girls. And fuzzy animals. And potted plants. But most of all I was afraid of the stock market. All those numbers got me confused."

In the next illustration, he asks everyone for help, including his mother, his rich uncle George, and his night school teacher. "I even asked my smart brother-in-law Murray, who doesn't even like me. But nobody could help," he concludes. "I felt lonely and dumb."

But then, in the next illustration, he's sitting in a big chair, and he's reading this very brochure from his company! "It explained how I could buy my company's stock real easy," he says. "While I'm saving my money, I can watch how the stock is doing. If it goes up, I can buy. If it goes down, I can decide not to buy. Best of all, if I don't buy, no one will be mad at me and I can get all my savings back with interest."

In the next illustration, he says, "I'm a happy guy now!" as he participates in a ticker tape parade on Wall Street. "Because buying stock is simple, thanks to my company's stock purchase plan. Sure, there's still some risk involved if I decided to buy the stock. But that's the way it is in the stock market. And I'm not afraid of the stock market anymore."

In the last illustration, he's about to come around a corner and collide with a tall woman, carrying a potted plant, with a fuzzy dog on a leash.

# The Beauty and Art of Illustrations

What's beautiful about using illustrations in describing savings or stock plans is that you can tell a story that summarizes the plan, its features, and how it works in captions. Even if all the reader does is look at the illustrations and read the captions, you've conveyed the basics of the plan and how it works.

We've often used this technique, and the results show that it works wonderfully. In fact, employees comment in surveys how much they like the fact that they can understand the plan simply by looking at the illustrations and then reading the captions.

# Personalize to Make a Point

The personalized print statements and online reports that many retirement fund managers provide have been invaluable to help employees understand how they're doing. But sometimes you need to go further than a simple accounting. The head of HR at a financial services company was concerned that employees in the lowest salary band in the company were not investing their annual award from a combination profit sharing and 401(k) savings plan—they were taking it in cash.

So we developed a personalized communication piece for employees earning less than $40,000 who were taking their awards in cash each year. The report showed "what you got" and "what you lost." For example, an award of $556 after taxes translated to $1,448 if the employee agreed to save her award and invest it.

The headings in this four-page printed piece were as follows:

- Don't Miss Out!
- Wait a Little, Get a Lot
- A Nice Tax Break

- Put Time on Your Side
- Take Charge of Your Future

In the "Put Time on Your Side" section, a bar chart showed what the projected value of the employee's account (this sample employee earned $34,500 a year) would be in two years ($4,681), five years ($13,756), and at age 65 ($232,469). The text explained that the numbers assumed a 3% salary increase each year and that investments would earn an average of 8% each year.

The text in that section began, "You may think you can't afford to save. Think again!" The text concluded, "Don't get left out—the deadline is fast approaching. . ." Then it told the employees specifically how to act to enroll in the program before the October deadline so that they would save and invest their award the following January. So we also had a little "just in time" communication working for us. The results? Fifty percent of employees did just that—they agreed to save and invest their award.

When we told the head of HR that a 50% response rate was fabulous, he said, "But 50% *didn't* sign up!" We suggested he talk with his colleagues in direct-mail marketing firms and then tell us how he felt about the results. He did, and then he bought us a bottle of champagne, which is always an acceptable and welcome way to say thank you.

# Checklist for Helping Employees Achieve Their Financial Goals

To make sure your employees save, invest wisely, and take advantage of every opportunity your company offers to invest in tomorrow, you'll want to do the following:

✓ Use every opportunity—even legally required communications—to encourage employees to save for retirement.

✓ Make it easy for employees to understand your savings and stock plans—through plan summaries presented by real employees or illustration captions.

✓ Share real stories of how people have saved and how they've spent their money. These are powerful incentives.

✓ Give managers periodic fact sheets with information they can share at staff meetings that will help employees sign up to save.

✓ Use personalized statements to sell employees on the value of the plan today and projected value for the future.

# 17

## Leaving the Company

*In this chapter, you learn how to*

- *Manage an employee resignation as you deal with your disappointment that the employee is leaving*
- *Fire an employee as gently and respectfully as possible*
- *Communicate during a layoff*
- *Ensure that the employees who remain are kept informed and feel valued*

## "You Say Good-bye, and I Say Hello"

And now we come to the end—of your relationship with your employee. We're devoting this final chapter to communicating departures—from a resignation to a firing to a layoff.

As always, our focus is on how to communicate, not on the legal, financial, and logistical aspects of separation. (Quite a few books have been written about those topics, including *Employee Termination Source Book* by Wendy Bliss and Gene Thornton, available from the Society of Human Resources.)

Here's a key point to remember: Although it's natural to focus on the person who's leaving, it's critical to spend just as much time and energy communicating with those who remain. After all, you want those employees to come to work tomorrow with a clear head and a positive attitude. You don't want them to be weighed down because of how a colleague's departure was handled.

In this chapter, we provide communication tips to help you deal with three ways employees leave: resignation, firing for cause, and layoffs (also known as a reduction in force).

# "Good News: I'm Resigning"

It's a sad day when a valued employee hands in her resignation. Even if the departing employee was not a star performer, a resignation brings unwelcome disruption. How will the employee's work get done in the short term? How will you find someone to take her place? What impact will the employee's departure have on the people she worked with?

As a result, it's not uncommon for people to feel angry that the resigning employee is "deserting us." And it's also not unusual for the employee's manager, HR, leaders, and colleagues to act out—to suddenly be cold, distant, and even mean.

This is not only juvenile, it's also shortsighted. Even though the employee is leaving (for what she believes are good reasons), the relationship continues, especially in the social-networked small world in which we live. A resignation is actually an opportunity—a chance to influence the soon-to-be ex-employee to have a positive attitude about her soon-to-be former employer. If the transition is managed well, the potential exists for the employee to do the following:

- Say positive things about the company's products or services
- Recommend her former company to potential employees as a good place to work
- Become a client
- Return someday to become an employee again, bringing the valuable skills she learned while she was away

So how do you handle a resignation in a positive way? Since these events are usually a surprise, we recommend that you prepare in advance by creating a Guide to Successful Resignations. Provide the guide to managers, either ahead of time (as part of a manager's tool kit) or immediately after an employee tenders her resignation. This guide obviously needs to align with and support your HR policies. Here's a sample of what this manager's guide might include:

| Stage | Steps |
| --- | --- |
| Receiving the news | Have a one-on-one conversation with the employee: <br>• Find out why he or she is leaving. <br>• Determine whether you can possibly retain the employee (such as by making a counter offer). <br>• Discuss the employee's preferred notice period and whether there is flexibility to extend this period (if appropriate for the group's needs). <br>• Agree on how communication with coworkers will be handled. (The employee might have close relationships with a few people whom he or she wants to tell personally.) <br>Consult with HR about open issues (notice period, counter offer, and so on). <br>If appropriate, have a follow-up meeting with the employee. |
| Managing the transition | As soon as possible, communicate with other employees in your group about the pending departure: <br>• Face-to-face is best, such as during a staff meeting, but if necessary, send an e-mail. <br>• Express regret that the employee is leaving, and offer thanks for his or her contribution. <br>• Articulate the transition plan. <br>Work with the departing employee to communicate with other key stakeholders: customers, clients, vendors, and so on. <br>Schedule meetings to transition the employee's responsibilities to colleagues. |
| Saying good-bye | Arrange a send-off appropriate to your company's policies and culture, from a pizza lunch to afternoon cookies to happy hour at a local pub. <br>Shake the employee's hand and thank him or her for all the ways he or she has made a contribution. <br>Wish the employee luck. |

# We Regret to Inform You . . .

Sometimes an employee just doesn't work out. Maybe the company or department isn't the right fit for that person. Or the employee doesn't have the right skills to do the job. Or the employee's attitude or approach creates constant problems. Whatever the reason, the employee's manager, with the support of HR, has decided that the situation can't be improved, so it's time to let the person go.

Even though firing the employee is the best decision for the company (and maybe, eventually, for the employee), it's difficult and painful. Still, it's important to handle the firing well, not just for legal reasons (no doubt you've consulted your attorney), but also because

- It's the right thing to do.
- Doing the right thing sends a strong signal to other employees that, even when things don't work out, the company still treats people with dignity and respect.

## Communication Principles

Our client, the head of HR at a global healthcare company, was facing a number of tough changes in the months to come. Because the CEO had introduced a new business strategy that required that many functions do their work quite differently, the head of HR was anticipating that a number of employees would be unable to handle the change and would be let go. Therefore, the head of HR asked us to work with her team to develop communication principles that would help guide how HR handled these situations. Here's what the team came up with that helped guide their actions throughout the transition:

- Develop simple messages using clear, concise language and a conversational voice.
- Focus on what is changing for the employees.
- Treat affected employees with respect.

- Be direct and straightforward.
- Explain why changes are occurring.
- Deliver information just in time.
- Provide opportunities for dialog.

## Quiet Communication

Communicating a firing should be as calm and quiet as possible:

- When you're ready (with all your documentation and the severance arrangement), have a conversation with the employee, preferably in a neutral location such as a conference room. Some companies require that an HR manager be present, along with the employee's manager. In any case, calmly explain to the employee why he is being fired. This is not the time for long explanations, just a summary of why the relationship is ending. The employee may want to talk or express anger or frustration. It's your job to listen for as long as the employee needs. Although feelings may be running high, try to end on a positive note, wishing the employee well.

- During the meeting, be clear about what happens next. Your policy may require an employee to leave the workplace immediately, or you may give the employee a day or two to get his stuff organized. Let him know how coworkers and others will be informed of his departure.

- After the employee leaves, or as he prepares to leave, communicate with others on his team or in his function. At Alison's company, we prefer a face-to-face meeting so that employees can hear the news straight from the boss. At other companies, especially those with remote employees, e-mail is used to get the news out quickly. Either way, you need to be brief, since you can't go into too many details. But we believe you should make it clear that this person was fired because he didn't work out, not because you were trying to cut costs. It's actually a positive thing when employees understand that your company will fire someone for poor performance: It sends a signal that your expectations are high, and that you won't let someone struggle who can't make a meaningful contribution.

### *"Let's Focus on What Happens Next"*

One of the best tactics we've seen in the manager/employee discussion where an employee is being fired is when the manager moves quickly to focus on what happens next rather than dwelling on what went wrong.

Here's what this sounds like:

"Tom, I'm sorry that your job here isn't working out in a way that's good for either you or the company, so we've decided to end your employment. You've been struggling with [name one or two job criteria].

"In this meeting, I'd like to focus on what happens next. You'll be paid through [date] and you'll receive xx weeks of severance pay, either in a lump sum or on regular paydays. If you take a lump-sum payment, your insurance coverage would stop immediately, so you may want to continue receiving your regular pay. You're eligible for outplacement counseling, which means you'll get help in finding your next job . . . ."

This tactic helps focus any discussion on what happens next rather than an argument about what went wrong, which won't end happily for anyone involved.

# The Worst Day Ever: Layoffs

It's sad but true that at many companies, layoffs have become a way of life. According to the consulting firm Accenture, 65% of U.S. companies reduced their number of full-time employees in 2009, and 63% of global companies did so.

But just because layoffs are commonplace doesn't mean they're easy. In fact, we find that they get more difficult every time, because they have a negative effect on morale.

We won't debate whether laying off people to cut costs is the right decision (although we will mention that one school of thought says that layoffs cause more productivity harm than financial good). We *will* tell you that there's a right way and a wrong way to communicate layoffs. We'll give you advice on how to do it right.

## A Good Layoff

A number of years ago, Alison was moderating focus groups at three manufacturing plants at the defense division of a large corporation. The company had put the division up for sale about 18 months before, and Alison's client (another defense company) had just announced it was acquiring the division. Alison was conducting focus groups as part of the process to develop a communication plan for the transition.

She began her first session with a group of hourly employees who built circuits for aircraft carriers. One of her first questions was this: "I'd like you to tell me about communication that has been effective. What made it work?"

The participants were silent. Sometimes this happens—people get a little shy about talking. But it's usually not the reaction Alison gets to this question, which is pretty straightforward and not very emotional.

She tried again. "I'm just looking for examples of communication you thought worked well. Maybe a meeting with plant management? Or a way you get news about how the plant is doing?"

A woman named Cindy sitting at the far end of the conference table raised her hand. "Yes, Cindy?" Alison said.

"This may sound strange," said Cindy. "But the best communication I ever experienced was during the layoff last year." The other employees nodded.

"The layoff?" Alison said, trying not to seem too surprised. She had heard that the company had downsized its divisional workforce by 20% to reduce costs in anticipation of the sale. But she certainly didn't expect employees to view a layoff communication as positive. "What made that communication so effective?" Employees in the focus group were eager to tell her:

- Management had made all its decisions about who would be laid off ahead of time, so the day the layoffs were announced, every employee knew exactly what would happen to him or her.

- Employees who were being laid off had individual meetings with their manager and HR, and they were given 60 days' notice. (By the way, this was before federal law made such notice mandatory.) They were then invited to stay on at work to help through the transition, but they were given the afternoon off so that they could process the news.

- Surviving employees then met with their supervisors to hear the news, and they were given the afternoon off as well.

- The next morning, the plant manager held a town hall meeting, which he called a "thank-you session." He explained why the layoffs were being made, and then he thanked all employees for their contributions to the plant and to the company.

- The thank-you theme continued for the next 60 days. Some employees stayed until the end, and others left earlier, but every Friday morning the plant manager bought all employees breakfast to thank them for their hard work and dedication.

"I won't say it wasn't tough," concluded Cindy. "But I appreciate the way they did it. Employees understood why the layoff was happening. We were treated like adults, with respect and courtesy. And the fact that management thanked us—that made all the difference."

## Experience Tells Us

Unfortunately, we've communicated enough layoffs that we've developed a tried-and-true approach for doing so. Here are the key strategies we find work well:

- Use face-to-face communication to deliver decisions that have a personal impact.
- Provide key leaders, including facility and functional leaders, with the support they need to be visible and effective.
- Prepare HR staff and managers to deliver communication.
- Develop print and online vehicles to deliver detailed information and reinforce changes.
- Consistently measure results and adjust your plans.

### You Need a Plan

As a first step, you need a plan. Effective layoffs require split-second timing, because you have many moving parts to manage. So you need to make sure you've mapped out all the things you need to do. The following is the first draft of a plan we created for a company that was making an acquisition. The company planned to announce large-scale layoffs to close a major facility as soon as the deal closed. We used the following timeline as a discussion document to work through issues and develop a more detailed plan:

#### Before Day One

**Selected executives/employees may be notified and immediately released.**

#### Day One

| Time | Event | People Affected | Issues to Discuss |
|------|-------|-----------------|-------------------|
| 8:30 a.m. | Managers arrive at work and are invited to manager briefing at 9 a.m. | All employees | What time do managers typically arrive at work? |
|  | Employees arrive at work and are invited to town hall meeting to begin at 10:00 a.m. | | |
| Morning | Employees who will be released immediately will be notified after town hall meeting. | | |

## Day One

| Time | Event | People Affected | Issues to Discuss |
| --- | --- | --- | --- |
| 9 a.m. | Manager briefing to give managers a heads-up on what employees will learn at town hall meeting | Managers | Who answers the phone on Day One? |
| 10 a.m. | All-hands town hall meeting to announce:<br>• Change of ownership<br>• Closing of facility<br>• How employees are affected (the big picture)<br>• Transition process | All employees | |
| 10:15 a.m. | Functional meetings:<br>• Led by managers<br>• Announce transition plan for function<br>• Answer questions<br>• Provide employees with appointment time and location for notification meetings | Employees by function | Ensure that managers are prepared for tough questions and for security concerns.<br>What is the role of HR in these meetings?<br>How will remote employees participate/be informed? |
| 11:30 a.m. to 5:30 p.m. | Notification meetings begin for employees who will be given a work-through date | Affected employees | Combination of individual and group meetings? |

*Day Two*

| Time | Event | People Affected | Issues to Discuss |
|---|---|---|---|
| 8:30 a.m. to 5:30 p.m. | Notification meetings continue for employees with a work-through date | Affected employees | |

*Day Three*

| Time | Event | People Affected | Issues to Discuss |
|---|---|---|---|
| Morning | Functional managers hold staff meetings with their teams to focus on next steps | Employees by function | |
| 8:30 a.m. to 5:30 p.m. | Notification meetings continue for employees with a work-through date | Affected employees | Goal is to complete most of notification by end of Day Three |

*Day Four*

| Time | Event | People Affected | Issues to Discuss |
|---|---|---|---|
| 8:30 a.m. to 5:30 p.m. | HR Admin Center opens to provide support for transitioning employees | | |

## Supporting Leaders Through the Layoff

Who decides to lay off employees? In almost every case, company leaders—and they're often the ones who decide *who* will be let go. But just because leaders are very involved in planning the layoff doesn't mean they're ready to communicate. That's why we recommend holding a briefing session to do the following:

- Help leaders understand their communication role, and prepare them to fulfill that role.
- Make sure they agree on key messages.
- Give leaders a chance to practice delivering those messages.
- Talk through potential situations that may occur.
- Vent about their emotions concerning the layoff. (After all, leaders feel bad too, and they need to work through how they feel so that they can get past it and focus on employees' needs.)

## When a Reorganization Leads to a Layoff

A consumer products company was restructuring a division that had about 10,000 employees to make operations more efficient. As a result, the company planned to lay off several hundred employees. To prepare leaders to communicate the change, we facilitated a half-day briefing session for the top 150 leaders. It was designed to help senior leaders understand and discuss the impact of the changes, as well as improve their communication skills. The session included the following:

- A presentation by the president of the division about why the restructuring was occurring and how it would be managed
- Small-group Q&A sessions with senior management so that leaders could work through questions employees might ask
- A quick session on how people experience change, focusing on the emotions employees were likely to experience
- An opportunity to practice communicating about the restructuring, to prepare leaders for team meetings they would hold during the next several days

**The result:** Leaders indicated that the session was a valuable use of their time. Their feedback indicated that they felt prepared to discuss the changes with their teams and understood the strategy.

## Managers Need the Most Help

Although leaders are responsible for communicating the big picture, it's managers who are usually on the front lines of a layoff. Even if managers are not delivering the bad news, they're the ones who have to deal with the aftermath of depressed departing employees and disgruntled survivors.

In our minds, there's no such thing as overpreparing managers for an upcoming layoff. In fact, we find that the more time you can invest in managers, the more invested managers feel in the change—and the more prepared they are to help employees through it.

## A Case for FAQs

In Chapter 8, "Make Meetings Meaningful—and Support Managers," we mention the importance of frequently asked questions as one of the most valuable tools to help managers communicate. When it comes to a layoff, we find that FAQs are a must—particularly for managers, but also for HR and leaders. Creating a FAQ document helps you work through all the issues involved in a layoff and helps you decide how you will handle these issues.

The key to developing an effective FAQ document is to brainstorm every tough question a manager or employee would ask, and then create a straightforward answer for each question. FAQs may then be used for leader and manager briefings, but we don't recommend that they be shared with employees directly. FAQs help prepare managers (who want to feel confident that they know the answer to every possible question), but they overwhelm departing employees. If you want to create information to give employees, develop a summary document that spells out the terms of the separation. This approach is consistent with what we advocate for communicating any policy or benefit: Give employees an easy-to-read and easy-to-understand print piece that they can share with family and that will help them make good decisions.

## Hundreds of Questions, and Their Answers

When we were helping a company manage a layoff last year, we developed a FAQ document that contained hundreds of questions to deal with every possible situation that could arise. Here's just a sampling of the questions that were included:

- Why was I laid off?
- What was the process for deciding who would be laid off?
- What job-related criteria were used in the selection process?
- How many employees are affected?
- When is my last day of employment?
- When is my last day on payroll?
- Am I expected to work until my last day?
- What if I want to leave the company immediately or before my separation date?
- What will my role/responsibilities be until my last day?
- Whom will I report to until the end of my service?
- Am I eligible to apply for a job at one of the company's other locations?
- Will outplacement services be available to me? Now or after my last day?
- Who is the outplacement provider?
- What services does outplacement provide? Will training be offered as part of outplacement?
- Will the company give me a reference?
- If I get a job at another company, can I encourage my coworkers here to come work at my new company?
- When should I file an unemployment claim?
- When can I begin collecting unemployment benefits?
- Will I receive severance? How much will I receive?
- Can I apply for and receive unemployment benefits at the same time I'm receiving severance?

- What will happen to my benefits?
- Will my employee contributions for insurance continue to be deducted from my pay while I'm still on the payroll?
- What happens to unpaid and outstanding health insurance claims (medical, dental, vision)?
- If I am currently not enrolled for company medical, dental, and vision coverage on my separation date, may I enroll after my separation date? Does this apply if I leave earlier?
- What is COBRA? Am I eligible for it?
- What kind of COBRA support will I receive after I sign my severance agreement or after my separation date?

*Give Managers a Chance to Practice*

The most effective way to prepare managers for an upcoming layoff is to hold a training session so managers get a chance to rehearse what they need to do. A key element of this practice is to deal with potential scenarios they might encounter during the course of the layoff period.

For example, the following are some scenarios we created for the company that was closing a facility after an acquisition. Employees were to be given notice and then continue working for 30 to 60 days to support the transition. We created scenarios that managers might encounter during this transition, and we gave them a chance to come up with potential solutions. If they got stuck, the session leader would help them develop strategies for managing these tough situations:

- An employee is disrupting the work environment with repeated outbursts. This individual complains to everyone about losing his job and expresses fears about finding future employment.
- Your team members seem confused about what they need to do. Some spend their time focusing on things that aren't important. Critical tasks aren't being completed.

- You can't get anyone to talk during your team meetings. Everyone has a stony look and won't join the conversation.

- Anytime you ask a particular team member to complete a task, he assures you he'll do it. But you've come to realize that he never follows through on your requests, and his work isn't getting done.

- The former manager of your group asks you a series of tough questions, and you're unsure of the best way to respond. You're concerned that the answers to some of her questions are tough to hear and won't be well received. In addition, there's one question you don't have an answer for, but you don't want her to think you're not in the loop.

# Checklist for Communicating as Employees Leave the Company

✓ Create communication plans for employees who are leaving, as well as those who are staying.

✓ Share bad news in person. Focus on what will happen next and what transition help employees will receive.

✓ Encourage managers and executives to thank departing employees for their contributions, and treat these employees with dignity and respect.

✓ Prepare managers to handle transitions effectively through training, practice sessions, and coaching, and then give them "just in time" FAQ documents.

✓ Create a communications plan as a chart showing who will learn what, when, and how.

✓ Remember that endings are always opportunities for new beginnings. (We wanted our last bit of advice in this book to be cheerful. Thanks for reading. We wish you good luck with all your human resources communications, from recruiting to leaving the company.)

# Endnotes

## Introduction

1. "Study of Employee Benefits: 2007 & Beyond." www.prudential. com/.../StudyofEmployeeBenefits_2007andbeyond.pdf
2. "8th Annual Study of Employee Benefits Trends." www. whymetlife.com/trends/downloads/MetLife_EBTS09.pdf
3. "The Cost of Paying Attention: How Interruptions Impact Knowledge Worker Productivity." www.basex.com/web/tbghome.nsf/ 23e5e39594c064ee852564ae004fa010/ea4eae828bd411be852574 2f0006cde3/$FILE/CostOfNotPayingAttention.BasexReport.pdf
4. J.D. Power and Associates 2008 National Health Insurance Plan Study$^{sm}$

## Chapter 1

1. Saul D. Alinsky, *Rules for Radicals*, Vintage, 1989.
2. David K. Foot and Daniel Stoffman, *Boom, Bust & Echo: How to Profit from the Coming Demographic Shift*, Saint Anthony Messenger Press and Franciscan, 1997.

## Chapter 2

1. www.answers.com/topic/customer-profiles

# Chapter 5

1. Richard Saul Wurman, *Information Anxiety*, Doubleday, 1989.
2. Chip Heath and Dan Heath, *Made to Stick*, Random House, 2007.

# Chapter 6

1. Paul Martin Lester, Ph.D., "Syntactic Theory of Visual Communication," http://commfaculty.fullerton.edu/lester/writings/viscomtheory.html
2. Dan Roam, *The Back of the Napkin: Solving Problems and Selling Ideas with Pictures*, Portfolio, 2008.

# Chapter 7

1. www.bsu.edu/benefacta/article/0,,46305—,00.html
2. www.webpronews.com/blogtalk/2007/06/29/the-definition-of-social-media

# Chapter 10

1. Terence E. Deal and Allan A. Kennedy, *Corporate Cultures: The Rites and Rituals of Corporate Life*, Basic Books, 2000.

# Chapter 14

1. Daniel H. Pink, *Drive: The Surprising Truth About What Motivates Us*, Riverhead, 2009.

# Chapter 16

1. The 2010 Retirement Confidence Study, Employee Benefit Research Institute, March 2010, www.ebri.org/publications/ib/index.cfm?fa=ibDisp&content_ id=4488

# INDEX

## Numbers

1-3-9-27 formula, 65-67
401(k) plans, employee
  demographics and participation
  rates, 17

## A

action, emphasizing, 211-212
age demographics, 18
agendas for meetings, 122-124
"An Alternative to Performance
  Appraisal" (Van Slyke), 246
analyzing survey results, 145-147
*The Art of Facilitation* (Hunter,
  Bailey, and Taylor), 128
asking questions, 40-41
assessing current state of
  employee understanding, 33
attitudes of employees, 4
award-winning communications,
  writing, 47-49

## B

*The Back of the Napkin*
  (Roam), 86
Bailey, Anne, 128
benefits communication, 197-198
  benefit headlines, 73-74

describing benefits for job
  candidates, 162
emphasizing action, 211-212
employee needs, 199
measuring effectiveness of,
  212-213
objectives, 198-199
planned approach, 201
time management, 206-209
tips for clear communication,
  202-204
tools, 209-210
Walnut case study, 200-210
benefits survey example, 148
Berra, Yogi, 88
billboards, 110
Bliss, Wendy, 263
*Boom, Bust & Echo: Profiting
  from the Demographic Shift in
  the 21st Century* (Foot), 14
breakdowns in HR
  communication, causes of, 3-5
*Breaking Robert's Rules: The New
  Way to Run Your Meeting, Build
  Consensus, and Get Results*
  (Susskind and Cruikshank), 128
budgeting, 50-52
bulletin boards, 110-114

describing communication
projects, 49-50
discussion guides, developing for
focus groups, 23-25
distributing HR communication
projects, 46
*Drive* (Pink), 216

# E

e-mail
graphic e-mail, 106-107
pros and cons, 102
quantity of, 105
writing tips, 105-106
effective writing
chunking content, 75-78
concrete communication, 81-83
conveying what matters most to
employees, 70-72
emphasizing "how to," 72-75
explained, 69-70
headlines, 73-74
plain language, 79-81
readability, 80-81
effectiveness, measuring, 135
dimensions of communication
effectiveness, 136-138
of benefits communication,
212-213
of employee handbooks, 194
surveys, 138-148
elevator speech, 57
eliminating jargon, 79-81
emphasizing
action, 211-212
"how to," 72-75

employee demographics
age, 18
case study: demographic
analysis, 15-16, 20-21
defined, 13
explained, 11-12
and 401(k) participation rates, 17
geography, 16-17
importance of, 12-13
key employee demographics,
13-14
salary, 19
years of service, 17
employee handbooks
avoiding legalese in, 191-192
content, 187
Davis & Company case study,
184-185
encouraging employees to
use, 193
explained, 183-184
financial services firm example,
188-189
measuring results, 194
objectives, 186
organizing, 187-190
researching needs of, 186
table of contents and index,
190-191
titles, 193
writing tips, 191-192
employee photos, 94
*Employee Termination Source
Book* (Bliss and Thornton), 263
employees
attitudes, 4
communication needs of, 56

# M

*Made to Stick* (Heath and
Heath), 79
making it easy for employees to
do the right thing, 36-37
Managed Disability Program, 36
managers
communication needs of, 56
helping managers talk about pay,
222-225
role in employee orientation,
170-172
role in performance
management, 244-247
supporting, 130-132
supporting through layoffs,
275-278
managing
HR communication projects,
44-45
*measuring, 46*
*planning, 46*
*research, 45*
*time requirements, 46-47*
*writing and distribution, 46*
meetings, 125-126
performance. *See* performance
management
time, 206-209
measuring effectiveness, 46, 135
dimensions of communication
effectiveness, 136-138
of benefits communication,
212-213
of employee handbooks, 194
surveys
*analyzing results of, 145-147*

*benefits survey example, 148*
*buy-in and participation,*
*143-144*
*communicating results of,*
*147-148*
*conducting, 144-145*
*focus, 138-139*
*methods, 139-140*
*survey fatigue, 142-143*
*survey questions, 140-143*
"meeting in a box," 131-132
meetings, 119-120
agendas, 122-124
common mistakes, 120-121
expectations, 124
facilitation approach, 126-128
managing information sharing,
125-126
"meeting in a box," 131-132
objectives, 121
Web meetings, 128-129
message, framing
chunking content, 75-78
communication needs of senior
managers versus employees, 56
explained, 55-57
high concept, 57-60
inverted pyramid, 61-64
1-3-9-27 formula, 65-67
Millennials, 12
Miller, Arthur, 110
Miller, Eric, 90
*Moderating Focus Groups: A*
*Practical Guide for Group*
*Facilitation* (Greenbaum), 22
Monsanto, 162
Morgan, David L., 22

conveying what matters most to
employees, 70-72
emphasizing "how to," 72-75
explained, 69-70
headlines, 73-74
plain language, 79-81
readability, 80-81
Wurman, Richard Saul, 78

## Y-Z

years of service, employee
demographics, 17
*Your Attention, Please* (Brown
and Davis), 95

Zoltners, Andris A., 177
ZS Associates New Employee
Orientation (NEO), 176-178